THE NON-HUMAN WORLD OF THOMAS HARDY AND KI. RAJANARAYANAN

DR. JAYAPRAGASH J

Made with ♥ on the Notion Press Platform
www.notionpress.com

To my beloved friend and mentor Dr. S. Ganesan

Contents

Acknowledgements *vii*

1. Introduction 1

2. The Non-human World Of Thomas Hardy And Ki.rajanarayanan 9

3. Conclusion 67

4. References 71

Acknowledgements

Words do not suffice to convey my gratitude to my guide Dr. A. Subramanian who has acceded to my request to guide me when I was desperately looking for a supervisor after the sudden demise of my friend and guide Dr. S. Ganesan.

My heartfelt thanks to my Professors - Dr. P. Marudha Nayagam and Dr. A. Clement Sagayaraj Lourdes for undertaking this research.

I express my gratitude to Dr. P. Madhusoodhanan, Associate Professor and Head, Career Development Centre, SRM Institute of Science and Technology for his support and motivation.

I am extremely thankful to my family members, friends and colleagues.

Acknowledgements

[illegible] guide Dr. A. [illegible] when I [illegible] Ganesan.

[illegible] Rajagam [illegible] gratitude to Dr. K. Madhusudhanan, Associate Professor and Head, Career Development Centre, SRM Institute of [illegible]

[illegible]

ONE

INTRODUCTION

Great literature emerges when a writer expresses the experiences of his life. The everyday happenings of people around him make a deep impression in the mind of a writer and come out with beauty in the form of literature. All great writers are much influenced by their societies especially by the people, the milieu, the manner and customs prevailing in the societies and so on. The impact of these influences in their mind finds expression in their creative works. As creators, they have a worldly, deep, broad and keen perception and express their experiences with others. In their attempts to express their personal experiences and emotions, there could be a fine blend of realism and imagination. The fine mixture of realism and imagination does not happen consciously or wantonly but it happens naturally. However, the creation is made out of the imaginative ability of the creators; the fusion of human life in their creations is not an imagined one. It is very authentic or genuine.

An individual is a product of the society in which he is born and grown and his way of thinking is influenced by the predominant attitudes of his society and the physical conditions of his surroundings. He is often influenced by the people around him and patterns of behaviour of those around him. Besides people and their behaviour, the socio-cultural milieu also exerts a great influence in the mind of the individual. All these influences may lead to kindle the creative ability of the individual and the outcome of these results in the creation of a great work of art. Though his creation is a blend of imagination and truth or real happenings, the focal point of his writing that depicts the life of man is not an imaginary one but reality. It is not only the individual's consciousness that determines his existence but also the collective consciousness of his society that plays a crucial role in his creation. The relationship between the social status of the writers and the subject of their writings reinforces the notion that literature is a product of the society.

Human beings are not part and parcel of nature but are products of nature too. The importance of the concept of place always evinces great interest in environmental studies. The sense of 'place' is a fairly elusive term that is difficult to define. The strongest and most enduring relationships described by men and women in this cosmos are based on place. Human beings are always identified with the places or the environments in which they live. In simple terms a place usually refers to a geographical region or physical environment or human community. Due to the burgeoning of industries and the rapid developments in the field of science and technology in the modern era, human beings become enslaved to the modern inventions and discoveries and lead a mechanized life completely ignoring the physical environment or human community. Human beings who once used to live in close harmony with nature fail to recognize the constant flux in their way of living and feel dissociated with the environment in which they are part of. As human beings become alienated from nature, they completely forget that they are a part of nature. In such a scenario, the category of fiction that focuses the relationship between man and nature or man and landscape or the fiction that gives importance to environment and its impact on people would enable us to understand the perfect example of literatures dealing with nature or physical environment or landscape. Thus, the novels of the two writers deserve ecocritical merits and attention. It is evident in the novels of these two writers that humans come into contact with the natural environments through various facets of labour, through the house they build, the road they travel, the field they cultivate etc.

Having been influenced by every aspect of their regions, Hardy and Rajanarayanan considered their regions as focal point of their discussion in their works. They were instinctive to adopt a largely rural perspective and depicted the tensions between the 32 simplistic or relatively free society without modern influence and the threats of progress, technology and societal conventions. They both had steeped in the rural culture of the world into which they were born and depicted the local life of the people and the harmonious relationship between man and nature with great precision and accuracy. Their writings express themselves as products of the nineteenth and twentieth century. Their influence from contemporary social and political issues and particularly the distinction between urban and rural life is quite remarkable.

Regional literature is the best medium to understand the peculiar traits and customs of people living in different regions. India has always been rich in its regional literature whether it is regional poetry, fiction or drama. Most of the regional fictions lay emphasis on place, beliefs and customs, mannerisms or behaviour and speech of a particular locality not merely as local colour but as significant conditions causing a great impact on the moods and behaviours of characters, their ways of thinking, feeling and acting. Both regional and local colour fictions are concerned with an accurate depiction of the manners, morals, dialects, and scenery of a particular geographical area. The regional novel is generally realistic in nature. It is a novel which focuses on a particular part, particular features which are peculiar to that region. As the regional novel depicts the physical environment, life, customs, manners, history etc. of some particular region or locality, it does not mean that regionalism is mere factual reporting or photographic reproduction. The unique features of a particular locality in comparison with other localities may also be emphasized. Through the creative ability and the proper selection and ordering of information, the novelist stresses the distinctive spirit of his chosen region and shows further that life in its essential is the same everywhere. The differences are used as means of revealing similarities from the specific and local to the general and universal. The selected region becomes the symbol of the world at large, a microcosm which reflects the great world beyond. The greatness of a regional novelist lies in the fact of making the region universal in its appeal. There have been many literatures that are impregnated with the life of mankind in varied forms such as the way life is reflected; the accuracy with which it is reflected; the various struggles that man encounters in his life.

Thomas Hardy and Ki.Rajanarayanan are identified as regional novelists for their unique portrayal of the regions - Wessex and Karisal. Wessex is partially an imaginary and partially real region created by Hardy and Karisal is a land known for its black soil and cacti forest portrayed by Rajanarayanan and other writers belonging to this land in the Southern part of Tamil Nadu. As all regional novels are noted for discussing themes and concerns of a specific group of people, this group is demarcated based on local dialect, speech, manners, culture etc. Regional novels place emphasis on common man and the themes are common place. The two regional novelists' works provide a true picture of the life of the people living in countryside that reflects the conflicts in the contemporary society. In general, their themes are universal in nature; the actions of their novels are set in regions which they knew well and which they believed would become an appropriate symbol for mankind and the world. In their novels, a closely knit community with their regions and the 10 regions' influence on the characters is vividly seen. Hence the two writers took painstaking efforts to demonstrate the world that Wessex and Karisal regions are a separate world in itself by giving archetypal values to the characters. The two regions are separated from the rest of the world that they seem a planet in itself, while the various heaths, vales, hills, and plains in Wessex and Karisal are so unique in their customs, languages, trades and terrains that they seem isolated countries.

The plots like the themes in the works of the two writers are chiefly universal in nature but they have a strong admixture of regionalism. Since the incidents in the novels are habitually regional, the action is always strongly flavoured by Wessex and Karisal atmospheres. The problems portrayed by the two writers are as true in their regions as elsewhere. On one hand, the plot seems to be regional and on the other hand the problem is universal in nature.

Thomas Hardy belonged to Dorchester, the southern-western part of England which was renamed Wessex and was immortalized by him. No other writer in English has made his or her region as popular as Hardy did. It is because of his immense love for his land and people. He was bound by an intense feeling of community, personal history and social custom with his region and it is evident in many of his novels. He must have had a strong feeling of belongingness with his family and region in his boyhood period and an intense feeling of apprehension and anxiety caused by the various social and cultural changes which certainly would have instilled fear in his mind as he grew up. Significantly, his desire not to grow up has been recorded in his biography The Life and Works of Thomas Hardy edited by Michael Millgate. It is quoted in the book that Hardy remembered lying on his back in a field, peering at the sun through his straw hat, thinking how useless he was and came to a conclusion that he did not wish to grow up.

Many writers in India have acclaimed fame and recognition mainly due to their portrayal of the life of people whom they know. Writers like Raja Roa, R.K.Narayan and Mulk Raj Anand have written with exquisite beauty and regional flavour in their novels. Rajanarayanan is one such writer who has achieved fame and recognition because of writing about the land and people whom he loves immensely. Ki. Rajanarayanan (1922 -) has played a pivotal role in the development and popularization of regional literature which has grown accidentally in the history of Tamil literature. The impetus to write about his village and people has paved way for the emergence of regional literature in Tamil. As he writes about the problems of the people who live around him, the lives of the people whom he is familiar with, his works are more realistic in nature than they are deliberately loaded with elements of regionalism. He expresses his desire of writing about his region thus: I want my creations to be in the same language as spoken by my people, in the same manner they think, the environment in which they live. It is my strongest desire to bring in my writings the smell of the air they breathe, the soil in which they are born, they wander, the aroma of the Karisal soil that emanates from their walking. I love this soil that much. (*Katturaigal* 125) This shows how passionate he is for his soil and its people. His affection and love for his land and his people is reflected in all his works. Rajanarayanan stands unparalleled in the depiction of Karisal land, its people and their lives. Even in short stories, he has the ability to create an experience of making the readers live with the characters that he portrays. Whether the central theme of his stories is related to a particular place or region or universal, he says thus in one of the interviews: "problems like poverty and hunger do not differ from one region or country to another. We portray the people of this region. Environment and other aspects are pertinent to this place. Only the setting differs" (*Ki. Rajanarayanan Pathilgal* 87). He is also of the opinion that the universal problems like poverty and hunger are depicted in the background of a particular region; the intensity of the problems does not lose its vigour. Such a plot can be just shifted to another region.

As there is a commonality between the two writers with respect to their perspectives in the transformation of the lives of rural people in their regions, an attempt is made at a parallel study of these two prominent novelists belonging to different nations, different races, different socio, economic and cultural backgrounds and different periods of time. It is noted that there are many striking similarities in the writings of these two novelists though there is enormous gulf between them culturally and linguistically. The literary works of these two writers prove the point that literature cannot be separated from other arts as art and humanity are inseparable. As the aspirations, ambitions and the reactions to failures and successes are similar everywhere, there are inter-cultural identities which make things easy for comparison. The words of Mathew Arnold in his inaugural Lecture at Oxford in 1857 have proved to be a remarkable flash of insight. He says, "Everywhere there is connection, everywhere there is illustration. No single event, no single literature is adequately comprehended except in relation to other events, to other literatures" (Mohit: 106)

As human beings are a part of nature or the physical environment, it is appropriate to say that they are shaped not only by the biological features but also by the environment in which they live. The surroundings or the social and cultural milieu in which they live determine the characteristics of human beings. There is a common saying that an individual is known by the company he or she keeps. This company encompasses the environmental and social company. Hence the primary influence of man is nature. There are many theories including the theory of Darwin that proves the influence of nature on man both physically and mentally.

One of the key areas in nature writing or environmental studies is to focus on the concept of place. Critics who belong to the school of ecocriticism reflect much on place in order to recognize the interconnectedness between history, human life and physical environments. Every writer has a unique kinship with the environment or the surrounding with which he bases his plot and makes his characters move around it. Hardy and Rajanarayan have attached special values to their regions Wessex and Karisal respectively. The world of Hardy and Rajanarayanan – Wessex and Karisal not only serves as a mere backdrop of their novels but also determines the action of their characters. Both the novelists give undue importance to their soil and its inhabitants especially, the non-human beings.

The scope of ecocriticism is mainly to create awareness among human beings about environment. Unless human beings make a conscious effort to understand the close kinship they have with the non-human world, the very survival of human beings is questionable. In the age of environmental degradation and global warming and ozone depletion, the emergence of the theory of ecocriticism has unified the scholars and the environmentalists across the globe to address the various environmental issues related to the extinction of our mankind and other non-human entities and also provide solutions to the environmental problems that the entire world is facing today.

TWO

THE NON-HUMAN WORLD OF THOMAS HARDY AND KI.RAJANARAYANAN

Thomas Hardy and Ki. Rajanarayanan are considered the most influential and inspiring writers of their ages and spent most of their time in rural regions Dorset and Karisal. Their harmony with Nature enabled them to have a thorough understanding of the natural world and motivated them to write about everything that they witnessed in their lives. Nature plays a pivotal role in their writings as many of their works dramatically affect the development of the plot. Therefore, their novels are rich in detailed and picturesque descriptions of the natural

The period in which the two writers started writing was marked by a lot of inventions and technological advancements, which resulted in new job opportunities in cities. The consequences of urbanization and industrial revolution were blatant in many rural areas. Industrial revolution had made a detrimental impact on nature and many writers were concerned with the vanishing traditional rural landscapes and countryside. The most significant writers of nature during the era of transition or urbanization are undoubtedly Hardy and Ki.Rajanarayanan who not only dealt with the beauty and wonder of the natural world but also the undeniable power of nature. Their portrayal of the natural world with all its inhabitants including flora and fauna and the relationship between man and the natural world is unparalleled in fiction writing.

To Hardy and Rajanarayanan there is a strong nexus between human and non-human lives in the realm of nature. Their writings would make the readers feel that man is either in collision or in agreement with the laws of nature. The perennial struggle of man with destiny controlled by nature is manifested in their works. Their passion in depicting the non-human world is as unswerving as nature herself and is as fresh as the repetition of the seasons. As Professor Panchangam rightly points out in *Rajanarayananjanarayanin Punai Kathaikalum Iyarkkai Ezhuthuthalum*:

Nature writing is not a kind of impression created by a work of art that carries the meaning of nature's language or it is not just the expression of nature by man but it is something that is to be observed minutely; it is not about making a pattern or structure of nature based on human perception, rather it is an infusion of man with the beauty of nature; it is a thorough observation of a natural scenery (Panchangam, 150).

These two writers have drawn close to the realm of trees, plains, mountains, rivers, birds and animals. Their intimacy with nature is almost uncanny. The intercourse between man and nature in the novels of these two writers is set forth with amazing power.

It is due to the spectacles the authors chosen to wear, they moved together in spite of differences in their culture. Having seen the intimate beauty of nature, they could not extricate themselves away from it. Their power of observation was sharp enough to capture even the tiniest things in the kingdom of nature with great precision and accuracy. It is this concern with the intimate relationship with nature that unites the two writers. For them, the mysterious power of nature and its message is not seen or felt in the unexamined, the untouchable, the dramatic but rather in the close and the small—the toad, the pigeon, the crow and the cow. Their writings propagate the fact that the non-human creatures are not to be approached with condescension but to be respected for the purposes of education. One of the chief tenets of eco-criticism is raising environmental consciousness of people. As eco-criticism calls for a paradigm shift from the anthropocentric to the bio-centric, the interplay of the human and nonhuman relationship is found much in the works of both Hardy and Rajanarayanan.

Like the deep ecologists the two writers were aware of the seriousness of life to all living creatures in the universe and shared the same feeling of compassion and love towards birds and animals. Nature is all pervasive in their novels. Their books are filled with the life and soul of man, animals, plants and trees. As ardent lovers of their regions and their beings, their affinities with the natural beings and people are commended and emulated.

The readers may be filled with a feeling of astonishment at the simplicity of the dramatic powers of the two writers. The delightful meadows and the rich lands of Hardy's region and the wildly grown cactus plants and the black soil with tall cotton plants of Ki.Rajanarayanan deserve special attention. The two writers emphasize on their works the protagonists' relationship with the environment and show the dependency of the human and the non-human relationship. This dependency between nature and men is what eco-critics analyze as nature writers do.

The novels of Hardy and Rajanaryanan are abundant with a rich source of nature imagery. As both of them were raised in rustic environments and they wandered for hours through the country side, there was a strong feeling of love towards all natural beings. It is this close involvement with the natural world that enabled them to have unusually sensitive feelings towards nature. When they were young, they observed the suffering of both animals and men in their regions; this probably would have ingrained in them a great deal of empathy for hapless beings. Their deep affinities with the farmland, animals, rocks, hills, valleys and the people who live among them are evident in their novels. This celebration of country life with all its merits and demerits has fascinated many readers of their novels. The personification of nature with humans and non-humans put them on the same level. The following part of this chapter focuses on the different roles of nature played in the novels of Hardy and Rajanarayanan.

Hardy's specific contribution to English literature is his original and unique use of nature in his novels. No other English novelist has even approached his complicated and aesthetic treatment of nature. His treatment of nature is sharply divergent from the conventional viewpoint and it is in direct contrast to the interpretations made by the writers who had preceded him. As he is a product of the philosophic and scientific rebellion of the nineteen century, his view of nature is completely different from the traditional perspectives as portrayed in the works of Wordsworth. Nature to Hardy is not something to be revered as the Romantic poets did. His characters never seek nature for solace and inspiration. He saw no mysticism in nature as Wordsworth did. The cheerful aspects of nature, the gentle and sublime are superseded by the severe and sombre in his vision of landscape, season and weather. Hardy perhaps speaks of nature's holy plan with contempt and stresses those features of the natural world that are antagonistic to man in addition to portraying the benign qualities of it

Thomas Hardy was aware of the dual power of nature – a nature of beauty and grace and a nature of ugliness and cruelty. One is the outside world of grass, animals, sunlight and flowers and the other is a sombre and vicious one. In his early novels, the readers could find a serene, calm and beautiful nature but in his later novels, nature loses some of its tranquillity and becomes a cruel, sinister force that causes destruction. Nature is portrayed not only as a mere backdrop in the sufferings of human drama but also a main character in his works. There are three significant functions of nature in his works. It functions as fate or causation for the sufferings of man; it is personified and it is used as an interpreter or delineator of characters' moods and emotions.

Hardy's novels are impregnated with nature images because of his frequent walks through the woods in his daily trip from Bockhampton to Dorchester. The walk was often in the dark when the uselessness of his eyes increased the keenness of ears. Through his ramblings over the hilly countryside he acquired lifelong familiarity with the winds and trees. As he spent much of his life communing with the lovely countryside of his birth, there is a realistic portrayal of nature without imaginative tinge as Hardy attempted to trace the beauty, charm as well as the ugliness of his country.

One of the sources of inspiration for many of his novels is the English countryside especially the Southern counties, villages and towns which he was familiar with and loved as a child. Many of the most beautiful descriptions of nature found in his works are a vivid recollection of this countryside. Hardy's vision of nature is the most characteristic manifestation of his creative power, and it dominates every scene of his novels. Nature and past are the first impressions upon a mind that is usually sensitive to surroundings. Wandering over the heath behind the cottage or through the woodland or among the apple orchards and corn fields and upon the lush, placid dairy farms in hamlets and villages, Hardy was sensitive not only to the tranquillity of the atmosphere but also to the rivalry and the struggle of animal and vegetable life. The beauty and wonder of nature and its cruelty towards mankind made a deep impression in his mind and a sense of ambivalence in his writings.

The plot of *Far from the Madding Crowd* is set in the area around Weatherbury. The chief protagonist of the novel Gabriel Oak falls in love with Bathsheba Everdene but she does not reciprocate his love and rejects his offer to marry him. She inherits a sheep farm in the village of Weatherbury from her uncle. Meanwhile, Gabriel faces a great misfortune in his life through the death of his flock of sheep which are killed by his dog and his hope of becoming a farm owner is shattered into pieces. After the loss, he moves to Dorchester and works in a fair but does not succeed. When he is on his way to another work fair, he lends a helping hand to extinguish the fire in a farm without knowing that the farmer owner is Bathsheba Everdene, his former love. Later, when her flock of sheep is diseased after consuming a weed, Oak comes to the rescue of the sheep and makes Bathsheba realize that he is worthy of being hired.

It is indeed Bathsheba's caprice prompts her to send an anonymous valentine to a neighbouring landowner Boldwood. His curiosity and emotions are aroused by the valentine sent by her. She rejects Boldwood's offer too but he vows to pursue her until she agrees to marry him. After rejecting the first two marriage offers, Bathsheba is captivated by the third suitor Sergeant Francis Troy who with his flattery, insouciant life and scarlet uniform wins her heart. Troy has already had an affair with a maid named Fanny Robin and he has to leave her because of miscommunication in the time and place where they were to be married. During this time, he courts Bathsheba and marries her. After a few months, Fanny, Troy's abandoned victim dies in childbirth. When Bathsheba comes to know the truth that Fanny is Troy's first love, she is stunned. In the same way, Troy is also surprised by the death of Fanny. Bathsheba is remorseful that she is indirectly responsible for the death of the maid.

Meanwhile, Troy is washed away by a storm when he goes to place flowers at the burial place of Fanny. When everyone accepts the circumstantial evidence of Troy's death, Bathsheba knows intuitively that he is alive. Troy does return, over a year later, just as Boldwood, almost mad, is trying to exact Bathsheba's promise that she will marry him six years later, when the law can declare her legally widowed. Troy returns and interrupts the Christmas party that Boldwood is giving. The infuriated Boldwood shoots him. Troy is buried beside Fanny, his wronged love. Gabriel, who has served Bathsheba patiently and loyally all this time, marries her at the story's conclusion.

Though *Far from the Madding Crowd* is Hardy's fourth novel, it is the first novel to be set in the semi-fictional land of Wessex. The plot of the novel is set in the second half of the 19th century. The nature that Hardy knew and loved as a young boy is predominant in this novel but his perception of it changed completely as he grew up. During his boyhood days, he admired the magnitude and power of nature. He gradually came to realize that nature serves mankind not only as a friend but also as a ruthless monster. This realization of the twin forces of nature caused a great impact on his description of it and the way it was portrayed in numerous occasions in his stories.

The novel begins with a facile and gentle description of nature. The opening scene establishes an image of a serene, beautiful and colourful day with Bathsheba's wagon wandering through the fields and Gabriel is unseen but observant. The whole scene is steeped in colour and sunlight. The whole atmosphere is saturated with warm summer breeze blowing through the valley which evokes a delightful feeling of beauty and safety. After a short while, Hardy slowly shifts the setting to Norcombe Hill which completely lacks pastoral elements. It is not a place of tranquillity and beauty but a place of desolation, sadness and gloominess. By setting a desolate scene of Norcombe Hill, Hardy exhibits the ruthlessness and darker aspects of nature.

The hill was covered on its northern side by an ancient and decaying plantation of beeches, whose upper verge formed a line over the crest, fringing its arched curve against the sky, like a mane. To-night these trees sheltered the southern slope from the keenest blasts, which smote the wood and floundered through it with a sound as of grumbling, or gushed over its crowning boughs in a weakened moan. The dry leaves in the ditch simmered and boiled in the same breezes, a tongue of air occasionally ferreting out a few, and sending them spinning across the grass. A group or two of the latest in date amongst the dead multitude had remained till this very mid-winter time on the twigs which bore them and in falling rattled against the trunks with smart taps. (*FFMC* 57)

It is clear from the descriptions that Hardy does not describe a salubrious and happy place but a sullen and gloomy environment which is devoid of happiness. The grumbling and moaning of trees and the dry leaves in the ground indicate that the scene is set in late autumn or winter. In the whole novel, the author strikes a contrast between gentle and soft and hostile and cruel nature. The descriptions of the blades of thin grasses that cover the hill and are touched by the wind in breezes of differing powers and differing natures illustrates the twin faces of nature. One is like a soft broom and the other pierces strongly and is likely to cause injury.

Nature in this novel determines the fate of the characters. It is presented as an impervious and inexorable force that determines the lives of human beings. The chief protagonist of the novel Gabriel Oak falls as a victim to the unerring course of nature. He loses his sheep to the relentless forces of nature in the guise of a dog which is considered one of the humblest creatures. Standing atop of Norcombe Hill, he sees a slaughtered mass of his flock of sheep lying in a heap at the bottom of the hill. His loss of sheep is the primary reason for Oak to encounter Bathsheba Everdene again. Thus, nature plays a vital role in the fate of Gabriel Oak. This incident evinces that man has no control over the forces of nature.

Again in another incident, the same inexorable force of nature that kills Oak's sheep paves way for confronting Bathsheba and also brings the two together for the third time. But this time, Bathsheba's sheep becomes nature's victims and she is forced to depend on Oak's dexterity to protect the meagre number of sheep that is left with her. It is again the supreme power that sends Oak to save the dying sheep from eating a poisonous weed. It is this incident that makes Bathsheba understand the worth of Oak.

Nature in this novel not only acts as an instrument of fate but also acts as a source of premonition to Oak who lives in communion with it. Nature is beneficial only to people who are attuned to the rhythms of nature and to those who show respect for it. This is exemplified in the novel when Oak proceeds towards his home and accidentally puts his feet on a soft, leathery, distended toad. He takes it up and thinks of killing it to save the puny creature suffering from pain. On seeing the uninjured toad, he places it again among the grass. Oak is aware that this creature is sent to give him a warning that something bad is imminent and he has to keep himself prepared for it. Such warnings of nature sent through humble or tiny creatures can be recognized only a man like Oak who is in perfect harmony with his environment.

The very next night, when nature appears in the grand aspect of lightning, thunder and rain, Oak reacts to the warning swiftly and preserves the loads of hay by covering them with a tarpaulin. A great understanding of natural environment is shown by Oak throughout the novel. It is due to this reason that nature is sympathetic and merciful to him. On the other hand, the descent of nature's fury on Bathsheba's hay is unparalleled. The lightning is "dancing, leaping, striding, racing around and mingling altogether in unparalleled confusion" (308). Like an avenging warrior, it vents its anger finally on a lone tree that is suddenly stripped down to the bark and burned to the ground. In this case, nature is described as a merciless creature with human characteristics.

One of the exquisite uses of nature as fate occurs in this novel. The action of rain through the mouth of the gargoyle at the church exemplifies the fact that it acts as an element of fate. Troy has felt remorseful because of his treatment of Fanny, his betrayed sweet heart. She has lost her life because of his neglect, and Troy visits her grave to show his contriteness by planting flowers on the burial mound. There arises a rainstorm after he has finished his mournful task and when he sleeps on the porch:

The persistent torrent from the gurgoyle's jaws directed all its vengeance into the grave. ...The flowers so carefully planted by Fanny's repentant lover began to move and writhe in their bed. The winter-violets turned slowly upside down, and became a mere mat of mud. Soon the snowdrop and other bulbs danced in the boiling mass like ingredients is a cauldron. Plants of the tufted species were loosened, rose to the surface, and floated oft. (375-376)

On seeing the results of the rainstorm, Troy feels that the world is against him. He leaves the grave and is next seen swimming out to sea, where he is picked up by a ship that takes him to America. It appears that nature does not have the facile and belated repentance, and washes out the whole of Troy's labour. This is not pure fortuitousness; it is nature's intervention.

Hardy again uses a storm as an instrument of fate because it reveals the unworthy character of her husband to Bathsheba. The storm almost destroys Bathsheba's farm, but Gabriel Oak works steadily to save the wheat ricks from fire and from rain while her husband Troy sleeps in a drunken stupor. Troy is warned that a storm is gathering, but he does not have Oak's perceptions concerning the signs of approaching bad weather and ignores the menacing forecast. It is Gabriel Oak and not Troy who protects Bathsheba's ricks from rain. When he tries to protect the rick from lightning from all the directions, he seems to be almost blinded by the flashes of light and the thunder crashes out of the sky with "a stupefying blast, harsh and pitiless, and it fell upon their ears in a dead, flat blow. ... A sulphurous smell filled the air, then all was silent and black as a cave in Hinnom" (309). Gabriel's fortitude and persistence in the thatching of the ricks despite an infuriate universe signifies the tragic choice that Bathsheba has made in marrying the alien Troy.

The correlation between landscape and the characters is exemplified in this novel. Bathsheba, the heroine of the novel meets her two lovers in two entirely different physical surroundings. The physical settings reflect the personalities of Oak and Troy. First, she sees Gabriel Oak while he is occupied with the ewes in the lambing season. On the other hand, she encounters Troy on a dark path and her skirt is caught by a sword. The activity of the lambing season illustrates the trustworthiness of Oak, his dependability and his concern and care for tender life. This is contrasted with the setting in which she meets Troy. The place is dark and overshadowed; so is the relationship of Bathsheba and Troy which is dark and full of disaster. The sword that pierces her dress is suggestive of the slashing of Bathsheba's peace and serenity in her marriage to Troy.

There are many images of nature used by the author to express the protagonist's physical and mental stature. In the opening scene of the novel, Hardy presents a much fuller and more impressive view of Oak, partly by seeing him at work and partly by associating him with the natural landscape in which he carries out his work. This scene is a night scene at a lonely place in late December; there are stars overhead and dead leaves under foot. A breeze is blowing and producing a sob and moan of foliage. A solitary man makes music of his own among the noises of nature. It is suggestive of Oak's gain in stature from his metaphorical association with this hill.

As a keen observer of nature, Hardy always had the ability to invoke in the readers as well as in his characters the specific moods he desires through the use of nature. When Fanny Robbin's coffin is brought for burial, the description of the fog that encloses the casket and wagon heightens the mood of sadness for the reader. Joseph Poorgrass is sent with a cart to bring the corpse of Fanny to the church. As the wagon rolls along the road towards Weatherbury, Joseph sees strange clouds and scrolls of mist rolling over the landscape. The mood darkens the whole scene and the fog hovers around Joseph like a spectre. Not a footstep or wheel is audible anywhere around, and the dead silence is broken only by a heavy particle falling from a tree through the evergreens. The dismal fog that comes down upon Joseph Poorgrass and his cart is felt unmistakably to be nature's silent commentary on the course of events.

Alongside of the benign and productive nature, Hardy places the vicious and unkind nature to make man realize that nature is an unpredictable force to an insignificant being such as man. The whole atmosphere of the book is marked by excess: a macabre death for Gabriel's sheep, a brilliant rainstorm threatening Bathsheba's farm, a drunken revel of farmhands undone by Troy's liquor, a garish coffin scene and a melodramatic killing of Bathsheba's husband Sergeant Troy by the maddened rival Boldwood. In these strong pages, nature is anything but mild and agreeable; it seems to be driven by the same energies and torn by the same passions that drive and tear the characters.

The action of *TheReturn of the Native* takes place across Egdon Heath on a November day when a wagon is driven by a reddleman

Diggory Venn with a woman named Thomasin Yeobright in the back of his wagon. Thomasin's marriage to Damon Wildeve is delayed by an error in the marriage certificate which makes Thomasin crestfallen. We soon learn that this error is perpetrated by Wildeve himself. He is infatuated with Eustacia Vye and uses Thomasin as a device to make Eustacia jealous. When Venn learns of the courtship between Eustacia and Wildeve, his own love for Thomasin induces him to intervene on her behalf, which he will continue to do throughout the novel. But Venn's attempts to persuade Eustacia to allow Wildeve to marry Thomasin, like his own marriage proposal to Thomasin, are unsuccessful.

Into this confounding tangle of lovers, comes Cly Yeobright from Paris. Clym is Thomasin's cousin and the son of a strong-willed Mrs.Yeobright, who serves as a guardian to Thomasin. Eustacia sees in the urbane Clym an escape from the hated heath. Even before she meets him, she convinces herself to fall in love with him, breaking off her relationship with Wildeve, who then marries Thomasin. Chance and Eustacia's machinations bring Clym and her together, and they begin a courtship that eventually ends in their marriage, despite the strong objections of Mrs. Yeobright. Once Wildeve hears of Eustacia's marriage, he again begins to desire her, although he is already married to Thomasin.

In marrying Eustacia, Clym distances himself from his mother. Yet distance soon begins to grow between the newlyweds as well. Eustacia's dreams of moving to Paris are rejected by Clym, who wants to start a school in his native country. Wildeve inherits a substantial fortune, and he and the unhappy Eustacia, once again begin to spend time together: first at a country dance, where they are seen by the omnipresent observer Diggory Venn, and then later when Wildeve visits Eustacia at home while Clym is asleep. During this visit, Mrs. Yeobright knocks at the door; she has come hoping for reconciliation with the couple. Eustacia, however, in her confusion and fear at being discovered with Wildeve, does not allow Mrs. Yeobright to enter the house: heart-broken and feeling rejected by her son, she succumbs to heat and snakebite on her way home, and dies.

Clym blames himself for the death of his mother; he and Eustacia separate when he learns the role played by Eustacia in Mrs. Yeobright's death, and her continued relations with Wildeve. Eustacia plans an escape from the heath, and Wildeve agrees to help her. On a stormy night, the action comes to a climax: on her way to meet Wildeve, Eustacia drowns. Trying to save her, he also drwons. Only through heroic efforts does Diggory Venn save Clym from the same fate. The last part of the novel sees the growth of an affectionate relationship, and an eventual marriage between Thomasin and Diggory. Clym, much reduced by his travails and by weak eyesight brought on by overly arduous studies, becomes a wandering preacher, taken only half-seriously by the locals.

This novel is again a portrayal of rustic life in fictional Wessex and is considered as one of the greatest novels for the description of a landscape Egdon Heath which is not only the physical setting in which the action takes place but also a main character that determines the destiny of all characters. As Charles Duffin states in his work on *Thomas Hardy:*

With the *Return of the Native* we are back on the Wessex ground: and this is in a special sense. The *Return of the Native* is a book of Egdon Heath; without Egdon it would not hold together. With most of the other novels the scene would be transposed to some other part of Wessex without vitality affecting the story: this story could not run its courses anywhere other than amid the solitudes of Egdon. (16)

The heath proves physically and psychologically significant throughout the novel. The weather patterns of the heath reflect the inner dramas of the characters. This novel is Hardy's critique of man's exploitation of nature in a setting where nature's inherent values are clearly seen. In this novel, there is a shift in the rhythm from the inhabitant's ability to read the signs of a coming storm to the need for a genuine love of nature for its own sake in order to survive in it.

The entire first chapter of this novel is devoted to the description of the heath which is presented as the most powerful agent to act on and for itself and it is in complete control. The opening scene of the novel is described thus:

A SATURDAY afternoon in November was approaching the time of twilight, and the vast tract of unenclosed wild known as Egdon Heath embrowned itself moment by moment. Overhead the hollow stretch of whitish cloud shutting out the sky was as a tent which had the whole heath for its floor. (*TRTN* 11)

The wild Egdon Heath has the ability to embrown itself moment by moment. The act of turning itself brown suggests that the heath has the ability to act itself and is capable of doing anything and it establishes a form of autonomy. Further, the author proceeds to provide a more specific description that the hollow stretch of whitish cloud shutting out the sky as a tent clearly indicates that the heath puts a barrier from which there is no escape for the human characters. The heath functions as a determinant of fate that constricts human life. Being dormant for years, the heath wakes up as a result of mankind's response to it. The opening scene of the novel itself is a clear indication to the readers that something is impending. Egdon heath is endowed with human traits. It is personified to show that all nature is dynamic. This is well illustrated when Eustacia walks through the heath "a bramble caught hold of her skirt, and checked her progress. Instead of putting it off and hastening along, she yielded herself up to the pull and stood passively still" (62). This manifests that the heath is not only made lively through descriptions of personifications but is also endowed with the power to hinder Eustacia's progress. The heath is at present a place perfectly in accordance with man's nature —"neither ghastly, hateful, nor ugly: neither common place, unmeaning, nor tame; but like man, slighted and enduring; and withal singularly colossal and mysterious in its swarthy monotony" (13-14). Though the heath is old beyond centuries, it is like humankind itself. It has all the traits of human who is neither good nor bad but remains an enigma.

The heath even has a voice. Treble, tenor and bass notes are found in it. The voice bears a great resemblance to the ruins of human song to Eustacia who has a strong desire to move out of it. The wind gives the heath a voice, a language. The ways in which the denizens respond to it are different from the way the characters respond to their places in other novels of Hardy. Though different characters relate themselves to their environments in different ways, the relationship between man and nature and man and place is taken further much in this novel. The heath appears to be a prison to Eustacia and a place of liberation to Clym. In this way the heath is not just a character but a projection against which human characters are seen. Through the use of heath, Hardy has attempted to create a landscape which is both powerful and vulnerable.

A wild nature has been created in the novel that does not accept civilization but rather causes death to those who represent civilization. It is a wasteland which is almost unproductive to grow anything beyond the little gardens its inhabitants keep. "Not a plough had ever disturbed a grain of that stubborn soil. In the heath's barrenness to the farmer lay its fertility to the historian. There had been no obliteration because there had been no tending" (22). The heath denies cultivation which is so vital to the farmers. As there is no tending, it cannot be considered a powerless or lifeless land. The heath is a force more than the sea. It has been there before humanity and it will remain there even without humankind.

The heath is described as an entity that for years it has come to life at night when other things sink brooding to sleep. It does not show any concern to the problems of the world until civilization makes it first appearance. The heath has remained silent for years despite innumerable crisis. It begins to react only when it is acted upon.

It is claimed by critics that Hardy never doubts that it is the presence of man who gives interest and meaning to Nature. It is opined that nature becomes insignificant without the presence of humanity. Yet this is not to say that humanity is given a higher value than nature or that Hardy gives human precedence for exploitation.

On the contrary, it is claimed that Hardy's subject is never concerned with man alone or nature alone but it is always concerned with man in nature. Man and nature are equal to Hardy though nature seems less valuable without human presence; humanity is also less valuable without nature.

The heath appears to be stronger in darkness as it exposes the frailties of human beings. The true characteristics of other characters are revealed when the heath is covered in darkness; only the characters that live in close communion with the wild nature of the heath find comfort and are at ease. This can be illustrated in the scene where Wildeve and Venn play their game of dice. Wildeve grows more uncomfortable as the night grows darker and it becomes obvious that the game goes out of his way. When his lantern goes out, he is forced to collect glow worms in order to cast some light on the dice, and once again he loses the game. Throughout the game Wildeve is annoyed at the animals and insects that surround the two, and the second time when the heath croppers arrive at the scene, Wildeve throws a stone at them and exclaims: "What a plague those creatures are – staring so!"(236). Venn wins all the money Wildeve is holding for Clym and Thomasin, and Wildeve has no choice but to return home penniless. Wildeve is not comfortable when the animals of the heath come too close; he thinks they are "a plague". The only creatures of the heath, he can stand are the glow worms. The exploitable things of nature seem to be conducive in the heath to a person like Wildeve who has an intense feeling of contempt for the place. On the other hand, the one who loves the heath and its creatures wins the game.

Being comfortable in dark enables one to feel things that one does not feel comfortable at day time. This characteristic applies to several of Hardy's characters. Clym Yeobright, the name itself indicating a connection to light, has his eye-sight destroyed by the bright light he studies in. It is thereby also a contrast to darkness. Clym loses his eye-sight due to his extensive reading. Clym reads at night, when the heath is at its most powerful. This destroys his eye-sight, but not his other senses. In the dark Clym has to put away his books and feels what he could earlier ignore. He stops every attempt at bringing civilization to Egdon, makes the final break with his luxurious wife and takes up furze-cutting. In short, he reconnects with the heath and finds his happiness.

The outcome of several vital scenes throughout the novel is determined by what kind of relationships the characters have with the heath, with nature. Those that represent civilization and thereby seek to exploit nature to their own advantages perish and those that do not attempt to cultivate but rather love nature for nature's own sake survive.

Hardy has created two characters, in addition to the heath itself, who serve as his heroes and they work together with the heath in order to emphasise a love of wild nature at the expense of modernization through cultivation. Although the characters themselves are rarely in direct contact with each other throughout the plot, it is only Clym and Venn who live in symbiosis with the heath. Furthermore, Hardy uses Clym and Venn in order to underline how landscape can influence the workings of mankind as well as promoting the values of those who understand it.

The novel's principal human characters Clym, Venn, Eustacia, Thomasin and Wildeve have unique characteristics in which their relationships with the heath lie at the core. Both Clym and Venn have relationships with the heath that separate them from the other characters. Clym represents a struggle between a love of the heath and a desire to civilize through education; Venn is used to run interference against the characters that view landscape, and thus the heath, as something only valuable if it can be exploited.

It is Clym who knows the heath well and he is permeated with its scenes. He may be said to be its product. "His eyes had first opened thereon: with its appearance all the first images of his memory were mingled: his estimate of life had been coloured by it" (177). With this reference to Clym's intimacy, Hardy establishes a bond between Clym and the heath, at the same time indicates a set of values deeply embedded in his character. His connection with the heath is so intense that he loses his eyesight in order to reconnect with the heath, when his scheme to educate has developed too far. When Clym returns to England from Paris to open a school, one of the first signs of civilization in an otherwise rural community, the reader is warned that it will not come to pass. Book learning is not possible on the heath. The heath will not give way to civilization of any kind – "Civilization was its enemy; and ever since the beginning of vegetation its soil had worn the same antique brown dress, the natural and invariable garment of the particular formation" (14). The powers of the heath do not want Clym to succeed. The heath is not meant to be tamed.

The heath seems to be an uncouth and obsolete thing to many characters in the novel. Even to a farmer, the scene of the coming corn and the fly-eaten turnips is frowning. But for Clym, when he looks from the heights, he indulges in a barbarous satisfaction at observing it. Clym's relationship with the heath is at its strongest out of necessity. He ultimately gives up his dream of educating the masses. When he finally takes to furze-cutting, he is one with the heath as "Huge flies, ignorant of larders and wire-netting, and quite in a savage state, buzzed about him without knowing that he was a man" (254).

Hardy constructed a unique relationship between the character of nature and his human characters in this novel. These relationships enabled him to publish a novel that was both well within the confines of the highly popular pastoral genre of the Victorian era, and simultaneously a critique against that genre's romanticizing of the human exploitation of nature. However, references to ancient civilization, schemes of education and true love of landscape blend together, traces of the author's ambivalence between civilization and a love of uncultivated nature become visible. Nothing could be more fitting for an author whose life and works had been torn between the demands of the metropolitan and his love of the rural.

The brute creatures of nature is revealed as instruments of fate in the novel. The bite of an adder causes the death of Mrs.Yeobright. She crosses the heath to her son's home, seeking reconciliation with

Clym Yeobright. A helpless and bewildered figure, she wanders across the heath in the intense heat of an August day, when the sun has branded the whole heath with his mark. During her return journey, she collapses and lies on the ground near the path. “It was swollen and red. Even as they watched the red began to assume a more livid colour, in the midst of which appeared a scarlet speck, smaller than a pea and it was found to consist a drop of blood” (295).

When Eustacia leaves her cottage to her escape from the heath, it begins to rain and as she stands pausing at the door, it becomes so intense that all around her “the gloom of the night was funereal; all nature seemed clothed in crape” (353). She soon loses her way in the darkness of the night, and in the blinding storm, she wanders to the edge of the Shadwater Weir pool. The torrents of rain have washed away the retaining wall, and Eustacia, blinded by the wild lashing of the tempest, stumbles into the weir and is drowned. Wildeve who jumps into the boiling cauldron to rescue her is also drowned in the attempt. Thus the violent storm is directly responsible for the death of Eustacia and indirectly for the loss of Wildeve’s life. These are some of the illustrations of Hardy’s deep feelings and the recurrent theme of the incompatibility of man and his natural environment. The disruption of moral destiny with an air of nonchalance and uncomprehending nature is the leitmotif of his works. Weather, landscape and animate nature assume the guise of destiny and man’s life is either changed for the worse or destroyed by the haphazard tricks of nature. It is vivid in the novels of Hardy that nature shows no sympathy for human aims and that there is always a struggle between man and his environment. The nature he conceives has an omnipotent power and human beings figure only as puppets as directed and controlled like some powerless creatures in the hands of it.

As the heath has the power of life or death over all the characters, the characters’ reaction to it determines their destiny. Eustacia Vye is the most rebellious of all involved in the game of tragedy. The heath is a prison to her. She is at variance with her surroundings as she is an alien and yearns to return to those brighter lands from where she has come. "Egdon was her Hades ... She felt like one banished; but here she was forced to abide... Her prayer was always spontaneous, and often ran thus. O' deliver my heart from this fearful gloom and loneliness" (73). As she fails to subdue herself to the hands of nature and is rebellious, the consequence she faces in her life is death. Wildeve is yet another character that expresses his contempt for the heath and fails to understand the inner purpose or design of nature or the environment in which he lives; he also suffers the same fate as Eustacia does. His rebelliousness is not as intense as Eustacia's. Clym Yeobright, on the other hand, does not feel repugnant for the heath and so he finds solace and tranquillity. The inactive heath soothes Clym who has not been enticed by the vacuity and futility of life he has formerly led.

Clym does not defy the heath and so he is permitted to live and he finds his purpose and fulfilment within the expanse of its borders. He is the chosen son of Egdon. He is in sympathy with its moods and finds congeniality and amiability written in the faces of the hills around him. Egdon has been his cradle; he is permeated with its scenes. He finds immense delight in counting its denizens, the snakes, heath croppers and his friends. Above all, he loves the rugged face of the moor. He is bound in an intimate fashion to the heath by the ties of his relationship. His desire is to serve humanity in some way or the other. In the end of the novel, he is found as an itinerant preacher and lecturer. His acceptance of life and submission to the heath is rewarded with contentment. There is another character that also lives in harmony with this region and finds satisfaction in observing its haggard features, is Thomasin. As she does not revolt against the heath, she is rewarded with feeling of contentment and happiness. The outcome of several vital scenes throughout the novel is determined by what kind of relationships the characters have with the heath, with nature. Those that represent civilization and thereby seek to exploit nature to their own advantages perish and those that do not attempt to cultivate but rather love nature for nature's own sake survive.

The plot of *The Woodlanders* is certainly an uncomplicated one which is based on the conflict between social aspirations and class loyalties. This novel is primarily concerned with the Melbury family that lives in a secluded woodland hamlet where Mr.Melbury is a prosperous timber dealer. He has worked sufficiently hard to afford for his only child, Grace, the benefits of a higher education. Melbury has promised Giles Winterborne to marry off his daughter to him for making atonement of a wrong he has done to Giles' father years before. Giles is in the apple and cider trade, and although poorer than the Melburys, he is on good terms of social intimacy with them. He is silently worshipped by a young girl, Marty South, who works with him in planting and felling trees, and is intellectually, if not socially, on the same level. When Grace returns from her private school, Melbury realises that her education and acquired social refinements will all be wasted if she marries Giles. His attempts to foster an amity with a lady Mrs.Charmond, the owner of the most of the land and property in the locality, is thwarted as the pretentious lady does not care to be seen in the presence of the younger and graceful Grace. Melbury is delighted when Grace captures the attention of the young Dr. Fitzpiers, who is from an old, well-established, although now impoverished, family.

Despite his promise to Giles, Melbury encourages Grace to marry the unreliable doctor. Another obstacle to Giles' claim to Grace is his loss of the property of several houses in the village because of the death of one of their inhabitants, Marty South's father. The houses revert to the ownership of Mrs.Charmond and Giles is left homeless and practically penniless. Consequently, Grace is persuaded to marry Fitzpiers despite her misgivings about his fidelity. Shortly after their marriage, Fitzpiers meets Mrs. Charmond and the two become infatuated with each other. Grace knows about the affair but it does not cause her so much anguish as it does to her father, who realises that he has sacrificed his daughter's well-being to his own pride. Fitzpiers runs off with Mrs. Charmond to Europe and Melbury attempts to secure a divorce for Grace, thinking it will be an easy matter. He desperately wishes her to marry Giles when she is freed from Fitzpiers legally, and Grace is very willing. However, the prospect of a divorce proves illusory and some months later Fitzpiers turns up again after Mrs. Charmond has been murdered by a former lover. On his arrival in the village, Grace runs away from her father's house and takes refuge in Giles' small hut in the wood. She remains there for a few days, but in order not to compromise her, Giles refuses to share his hut with her and insists on sleeping out of doors, even though he has been very ill. As a result of this, he contracts a fever and dies, despite Grace's last minute attempts to save him by calling out Fitzpiers. Grace mourns for Giles, together with Marty, and refuses to live with her husband, who nevertheless persists in his efforts to win her back. He eventually convinces her of his sincerity, and she returns to him. Melbury is left bitter and regretful, and Marty South is left alone to grieve for Giles.

As in other novels, representation and personification of nature is rich in *The Woodlanders*. Hardy takes the readers to a land of apple trees through the portrayal of Little Hintock. The setting of the novel is made to stand for the universe and it has a symbolic value. It is not only a background but also an actor that is always present, the incarnation of a living force with a will and a purpose of its own now and then taking an actual hand in the story and killing the chief protagonist, Giles Winterborne.

The people of Hintock are completely isolated by the trees that they have planted so carefully. They are severed from the finer aspects of society in the outside world; but they are also guarded by the trees from hunger and cold. Hence the woodland of Little Hintock has a two-fold function. It serves as both a liability and an asset. Life in Little Hintock is as remote from civilization as is the life on Egdon, but it is not isolated by a heath but by trees. It is seen as a place of innocence, safety and natural fertility.

The natural world of Little Hintock presented by Hardy is completely different from that of Weatherbury in *Far from the Madding Crowd* and Egdon Heath in *The Return of the Native.* Though it is a wondrous world of sap and leaves, the more prevalent images of the place suggest it to be a microcosm of a world in which the struggle for existence is the chief condition of human existence. The novel is dominated by descriptions of suffering and torment that natural objects inflict on one another. This is well illustrated by the description of an elm tree that is the main sustenance of life and death of John South.

The trees of Little Hintock have their beauty but in some aspects nature is not life-sustaining or even neutral but actively hostile to human beings, like the tree that kills John South.

The tree was a tall elm, familiar to him from childhood, which stood at a distance of two- thirds its own height from the front of South's dwelling. Whenever the wind blew, as it did now, the tree rocked, naturally enough; and the sight of its motion, and sound of its sighs, had gradually bred the terrifying illusion in the woman's mind. Thus he would sit all day, in spite of persuasion, watching its every sway, and listening to the melancholy Gregorian melodies which the air wrung out of it. (*TWL*77)

Through the years, the tree has taken over a significant amount of the old man's fears. He faces the tree in stark terror, realizing that as the time passes, he is faced with a supernatural force that he could do nothing to combat. Mr.South wails and bemoans his enemy; for he recognizs the enemy as nature.

Ironically John South dies almost immediately after he learns the tree has been felled by Giles in an attempt to save South's life. He appears to have been destined to live only as long as his tree lived – and man and nature shared the same fate. When one dies, the other must die; just as they grow together, and they also end together. Thus, man and nature are bound together in twin destinies, each sharing the fate of the other.

Unlike the sombre, gloomy heath, the extensive woodlands in Hintock is interspersed with apple orchards. The forest is so dense that the sun cannot be seen until midday, and in some part of the wood, the continuous shade prevents any growth under the beaches, and always there is the constant murmur of the rustling leaves with the sound almost metallic like the sheet iron foliage of the fabled Jarnvid wood. Hardy uses the woodlands in a series of personified images as a means of extending throughout the universe the same suffering he sees in man.

The woodland is characterized not by repose and endurance like Egdon heath but by its struggle for existence. The trees must compete with one another and with the elements, parasites and animals in order to maintain themselves and to lift their branches triumphantly to the sky. The description of the warfare among the trees conveys man and nature's tragic situation. The summer shadows in the dense woodland are mysterious and frightful. In winter, the leafless trees look like a weird multitude of skeletons. In heavy moist weather the many boughs seem to be in a cold sweat. The trees and bushes are haggard phantoms under a still gray sky. On a violent night in the wood it is difficult to believe that "no opaque body, but only an invisible colourless thing was trampling and climbing over the roof, making branches creak, springing out of trees upon the chimney, popping its head into the flue, and shrieking and blaspheming at the every corner of the walls" (*TWL* 255). The images and similes that Hardy employs to personify the wood are always in term of human agony; this imagery is so vivid that there can be no doubt as to the tragedy inherent in the forest.

The idea of nature as "the ultimate causality" is illustrated in *The Woodlanders* by a rainstorm which is the direct cause of the death of Giles Winterborne. Grace runs away into the woodland to escape her husband and stumbles accidentally on the little cottage occupied by Giles. Since Grace is unable to go any farther in the rain, Giles insists her to stay in his house, and he sleeps outside in a rudely constructed hut. During the night Giles tries to protect himself from the weather, but "the rain, which had never ceased, now drew his attention by beginning to drop through the meagre screen covered him." (*TWL* 252). It is this exposure from the rain and dampness that is the cause of Giles' death. Here nature functions as fate in the death of Winterborne.

Tess of d'Urbervilles is the story of a poor village girl named Tess in the village of Marlott. One day her father John Durbeyfield hears that he belongs to the noble and knightly families of the d'Urbervilles. Rejoiced by the news of his royal lineage, he drinks heavily without worrying about his next day chore. In the next morning, he has to deliver the beehives to the Casterbridge market. On seeing the condition of the inebriated father, Tess, the eldest of the family comes forward to deliver the beehives.

Accompanied by her brother Abraham, Tess decides to go to Casterbridge market the next morning. On the way, in an accident with a mail cart, their beloved and the bread winner of the family, the horse Prince dies. Tess holds responsible for the death of Prince. She feels guilty and remorseful for this and wants to do something to purchase a new horse. Meanwhile Tess is being asked by her mother to go to the neighbouring village Trantridge to claim kinship with the d'Urbervilles. Forced by the condition of the family, she goes there against her will to work but not to claim kinship. A blind lady is the owner of the farm. She offers her a job at the poultry farm. There she confronts Alec d'Urberville, the antagonist of the novel, an affluent libertine who constantly proposes and seduces Tess and exhorts her to fall in love with him. One night, after a dance in the local town Alec tricks Tess into accepting a ride home with him. He gets lost in the woods and leaves to find the path leaving Tess alone. She falls asleep when he comes back and when she is in a state of semi-consciousness he seduces and rapes her. She cannot live there as a mistress at the cost of her chastity. She returns to Marlott. In tears she tells her story to her mother. In due course of time, she gives birth to a son, who cannot live long. His death helps Tess forget her past which always pricks her like a thorn.

After two long years she starts earning her livelihood, and for the second time she leaves her home for Talbothays and there she obtains a job as a milk maid. It is a very big dairy. In Talbothays, she falls in love with Angel Clare, the youngest son of an earnest orthodox parson of Emminster, the Reverend James Clare. His father is revered everywhere for his piety. As Angel Clare is much interested in humanity rather than divinity, his father refuses him education at Cambridge. The study at home has made Angel to be in love and generous with the low and the poor. He has determined to adopt farming as his career. He has come to Talbothays to learn dairy farming. As time passes the love of Angel Clare and Tess becomes more intense and deeper. Angel finds difficult to suppress his feeling, he proposes to Tess but she does not accept his proposal immediately. She always seems to be evasive in reciprocity of the proposal and says that she is not fit for him. Her past always lingers before her eyes. The keener the desire to expose her sins arises in her mind the feebler she feels herself. She does not want to deceive him. Even before marriage she writes herself a letter and slips it in his room, but the letter slides under the carpet. Finally, they marry. At the wedding night, Angel confesses a past mistake of his involvement with a woman senior to him in age, she too confesses her faults.

Dejected by this and unable to forgive Tess as she forgives him, Angel decides to desert her. Disheartened Angel also plans to go to Brazil. The paltry amount given by Angel before leaving for Brazil is soon finished and Tess again gets exposed to starvation. Due to her pride she cannot move to her parents and due to the fear of defaming Angel, she cannot accept indoor work. She works at a bleak starve-acre farm with Marian, who has started drinking since Angel rejected her. Tess randomly meets Alec d'Urberville again, but now he has become an evangelical preacher, converted by Angel's father. When he sees Tess, he becomes enamoured once more, and quickly gives up Christianity to try and seduce her. Tess goes home to take care of her mother, but soon afterward her father dies. The family is then evicted, and Alec offers to help them if Tess returns to him.

Meanwhile, Angel who has grown sick in Brazil, decides to come home and forgive Tess. When he finally finds her, she is in a fancy boarding house, and she says it is too late for her, she has relented to Alec. Angel leaves, stricken, and Tess argues with Alec, ultimately stabbing him to death. Tess and Angel then escape together, with Angel unsure if Tess actually committed murder. They hide in an empty mansion and have a few happy days, but then move on. One night they stop at Stonehenge, and Tess falls asleep on a monolith.

At dawn the police arrest her. Later Angel and Tess's sister, Liza-Lu, hold hands and watch the black flag, the sign that Tess has been executed.

Tess is often considered Hardy's one of the finest novels and it has brought him fame and recognition in the genre of fiction writing. Like other novels, this is also set in Wessex during the late 19th century. The impact of Industrial Revolution on the agricultural rural areas is vividly seen in this novel too. This novel contains numerous descriptions of landscape and natural world that are interwoven with the plot. Through the depictions of natural settings and surroundings, Hardy brings to light the fact that man is transient in nature where as nature is everlasting.

Nature again plays a vital role in the development of the plot as in other novels of Hardy. The various seasons portrayed reflect the different phases of the character's life. Unlike other novels, in *Tess* Hardy did not show his interest in exploring the interaction of a number of individuals within a community but showed his interest in depicting the physical and emotional sufferings of one single character, Tess. In this novel, nature imagery is no longer needed to assist in differentiating one character from another; it functions to distinguish and illuminate the psychological state of the protagonist. As life in nature is born in spring season, Tess's story also begins in the same season of the year. Her life becomes gloomy or miserable during autumn as she is raped by Alec. Her life calms down again and her passion for Angel Clare starts developing with the advent of summer. Again, their marriage is symbolically doomed from the very beginning as it takes place during a cold New Year's Eve. The different seasons used by Hardy indicates the correlation between the plot and the happening of various events.

Besides the influence of seasons in the action of the plot, the readers can also observe the way natural settings reflect the mood or emotional state of the characters. When Tess is at the apex of bliss, she and nature seem to be one: "Her hopes mingled with the sunshine in an ideal photosphere which surrounded her as she bounded along against the soft south wind. She heard a pleasant voice in every breeze, and in every bird's note seemed to lurk a joy" (*TESS* 91).

Tess listens to the sounds of nature and feels as if it communicates with it. The weather is in perfect symbiosis with her mood and mirrors the joyful atmosphere of the scene. However, when she contemplates on whether to accept Angel's marriage proposal, the world around her reflects her remorse and indecisions. Right after Angel leaves the scene, the sun goes down and on the other side of the sky a monstrous pumpkin-like moon arises and willows become spiny-haired monsters as they stood up against it. Tess feels guilty when she hides her past from Angel and it is again mirrored in the ominous dark landscape surrounding her.

Throughout the novel, Hardy continues to portray nature as a beautiful and stunning creature. During summer when Tess and Angel are beginning to develop feelings for each other, Hardy presents the natural setting in a very serene and astonishing way.

Or perhaps the summer fog was more general, and the meadows lay like a white sea, out of which the scattered trees rose like dangerous rocks. Birds would soar through it into the upper radiance, and hang on the wing sunning themselves, or alight on the wet rails subdividing the mead, which now shone like glass rods. Minute diamonds of moisture from the mist hung, too, upon Tess's eyelashes, and drops upon her hair, like seed pearls. (*TESS* 116)

The tenderness of the natural scenery seems to encourage their love as Tess's beauty is enhanced through natural elements such as the mist moist on her eyelashes and hair compared to diamonds and pearls. Nature seems to care about them being together, as a mother helping her children to find love.

Hardy's perception of nature in this novel is predominantly of naturalistic character. When Tess is escorted by Alec through The Chase, their surroundings are firstly described in a very romantic way. The calm, sleeping nature evokes feelings of peace and safety and welcomes Tess to rest in its arms.

There was no answer. The obscurity was now so great that he could see absolutely nothing but a pale nebulousness at his feet, which represented the white muslin figure he had left upon the dead leaves. Everything else was blackness alike. Darkness and silence ruled everywhere around. Above them rose the primeval yews and oaks of The Chase, in which there poised gentle roosting birds in their last nap; and about them stole the hopping rabbits and hares. (*TESS* 64)

Considering the fact that Tess is about to be seduced and raped, the quiet and calm depiction seems almost ironic. The napping birds and hopping rabbits and hares do not care about what is happening to Tess, there is absolute silence in the scene just as it would be in the woods right before the breaking dawn. However, this stillness of natural elements may as well be representing "the lull before the storm", thus, a suspicious sign of the upcoming chilling situation. Furthermore, the fact that the two characters wander through the woods named 'The Chase' could also imply Alec's ominous intentions. The only natural element that could possibly warn Tess about the imminent mishap would be the fog surrounding the place, crawling silently around them, coating the scene in mystery.

Although Tess is a pure countrywoman worshipping God and respecting natural laws, neither nature nor the Providence is trying to help her to escape such terrible destiny. Hardy, therefore, presents the indifferent and cruel face of nature, which has no mercy upon any living creatures. As mentioned, Tess has been presented as a woman in perfect harmony with nature, being even a part of the landscape; nevertheless, she is violated and changed forever. Unlike Gabriel Oak, whose knowledge of nature helps him protect the crops and prevent other natural catastrophes, Tess is left helpless. She eventually gives birth to a baby, who dies shortly after, but her life is already marked and she is judged by the society, as it is an unacceptable crime for a woman to have children out of marriage. Though she is in perfect harmony with the natural world, the divine providence or the world of nature fails to protect her.

Another moment concerning nature's lack of interest in human fate can be observed after Angel abandons Tess. Tess arrives at

Flintcomb-Ash farm during winter hoping for work. She is emotionally wrecked from Angel's departure and her despair and sadness are reflected in her current setting of the farm, which is described as a starve-acre place. Tess has to work in terrible conditions and the natural forces keep pushing her even further to the ground.

In the afternoon the rain came on again, and Marian said that they need not work any more. But if they did not work they would not be paid; so they worked on. It was so high a situation, this field, that the rain had no occasion to fall, but raced along horizontally upon the yelling wind, sticking into them like glass splinters till they were wet through. (*TESS* 250)

Hardy again shows the cruel face of nature, which terrorizes Tess and others while working on the field. In *Far from the Madding Crowd*, Hardy described wind as a mild force treating the grass and people gently as a 'soft broom'. On the contrary, in *Tess* he refers to it as if the wind was 'yelling' and compares the rain to 'glass splinters' stabbing the workers repeatedly until they are soaking wet. Nature does not stop the rain to make them comfortable because it is no longer presented as a mother, but as a natural force driven by its own rules. However, Hardy's stance towards the perception of nature remains disunited.

Tess is portrayed as a victim without any choice of free will, as everything she did and went through could not happen any other way and led to a miserable, already predetermined fate. Furthermore, Hardy's selection of Stonehenge as a place of Tess's final capture, after she kills Alec, appears very symbolic. Just as ancient civilizations brought human sacrifices to worship the unlimited power of nature, Tess has to do one final sacrifice to free herself from her past.

The setting of Stonehenge is presented as a beautiful, majestic and restful place with only a gentle wind blowing around through the scene. Nature seems to be hesitant about Tess, it is serene and very still, evoking the image of stability and peace. It invites Tess to lie on the warm and dry altar and accept her destiny. Nature again, in the final moment of the novel seems to be a comforting force, caring for her child. The monumentality of Stonehenge and its individual pillars are presented as if they support Tess not only physically, but also emotionally in her final moments.

In comparison to *Far from the Madding Crowd, Tess* shows more distinctively the presence of Hardy's influence of the Darwinian theories and his inclination to naturalism, in the sense of objective descriptions and the indifference of nature. Unlike Gabriel Oak, who could partially influence his fate by reading nature's signs, the characters of *Tess of the d'Urbervilles* seem to be left without the possibility of choice or free will. Being from poor and decrepit family, Tess is predetermined to have a miserable life. Although she experiences pleasant moments during her life, which may give her hope for happiness, her tragic end is inevitable.

The unseen powers behind the universe are presented by Hardy as an impelling force in the lives of men. When he describes the fields, the copses and the hills of Dorset, it is not as plausible and necessary background to the lives of his characters. The moods of earth and sky enter into human life, colour it and even play their part in the story. The profound influence of climatic and physical conditions upon the character is admitted, but it has seldom been used by imaginative writers with conscious artistry or psychological insight as Hardy did. However, faithful the transcript of natural scenery may be in many writers, seldom it makes the readers feel its connection with human life as it does in Hardy's works. His fine and most distinctive gift of psychological suggestiveness unite the readers with the mood he creates of nature. It is impossible to shift Clym and Eustacia to the settings of Little Hintock and Giles and Grace to Egdon Heath. Such shifting of characters from one setting to another may give a sense of incongruity. The association with the different environments reflects the inner personality of the characters.

Hardy's depiction of the nonhuman world with all the essential elements of nature performs a dual role. Description of nature not only serves to illustrate the world in which the protagonists move, but it also reveals the emotions and moods felt by the characters and the reader. The artistic use of nature has made him one of the greatest writers in English. His concept of nature and nature's role in relation to man was formed under the influence of such men as John Stuart Mill, Charles Darwin, Herbert Spencer and Leslie Stephen. As a result of the revolution in scientific thought that occurred in the nineteenth century, Hardy divested himself of all beliefs in the benevolence of nature. He became convinced that nature, if not actively malign, is indifferent to man's welfare. Unlike Wordsworth, Hardy did not conceive of nature as the projection of mysticism and divinity of a loving deity. Hardy saw beauty in nature but realized that such beauty was camouflaged with carnage and destruction. Hardy treated Nature in his novels in a conspicuously unorthodox manner, portraying it as man's enemy and tormenter. Man is never helped or aided by nature but is thwarted and destroyed by its cruel and inexplicable tricks.

The natural world of Hardy comprises birds and animals to show that man is no way superior to these creatures. Hardy viewed nature as a personality and a force in his writing as his impulse was to integrate man with nature. The unforeseen and inexplicable stratagems of nature impacting the lives of characters occur throughout his work. Because of his conviction that scientific determinism was the only logical view, he believed that man's life was governed by a series of chance happenings. Hardy's views on nature is completely divergent from the views of naturalists such as Emile Zola who is of the opinion that hopes of mankind are based on a perfect faith in the ultimate order of the universe, and on the belief that humans have faith in life and confidence in nature. Hardy looked at life in an entirely different manner. He found no such harmonious and reliable scheme governing the natural world. To the characters in Hardy's novels, chance occurrences in nature bring only sorrow. He is convinced with the fact that the unheeding and casual working of natural law inevitably brings ruin to man.

The non-human or natural world of Rajanarayanan is suffused with a variety of natural elements such as wild cacti forest with rare species of plants and animals, torrential rain and horrid weather. As in Sangam Literature and in the works of Wordsworth who painted pictures of the green fields, dales, valleys, lakes, rivers and rustic folks, there are various descriptions of nature in the writings of Rajanarayanan. These descriptions are so accurate and realistic that they display the strong and intimate relationship between nature and mankind. Just like the sensuous poems of Keats with the keenest perceptions, the readers could see, hear, feel, taste and smell the varied colours of plants, silky textures of leaves, the aroma of fruits grown in forest and the fragrance of flowers in the realm of nature and the buzzing of bees and chirping of birds. Rajanarayanan's love for nature is so powerful that it permeates every page of his works. While writing about nature, he records even the language of birds, animals and other non-human beings in the world of nature. His keen observation of the natural world does not confine with the mere portrayal of birds and animals, he evinces great interest in the behaviour of birds and animals and goes one step further to reflect the inner workings of the minds of birds and animals, the conversation of hens and cocks and the communication of dogs and cows. His knowledge about the variegated trees is astounding even to a botanist. He believes that the world of nature is so mysterious and powerful that no human could understand the depth of it.

Rajanarayanan treats nature with great zeal not to just show the magnificence or the wonders of nature but to show how it impacts the lives of human beings especially people who live in agricultural societies or rural areas. The world of nature and the world of man are the two great fields on which his works are based. Like the Sangam poets who described man and nature with great precision and accuracy, the readers find in the works of Rajanarayanan the harmonious relationship between man and nature. These two subjects are interwoven as warp and woof in the fine tapestry of his works. He has the power to unite the phenomena of external nature with an insight into human feelings as either influenced or affected by them. His novels are related to land just like Sangam

Literature that focuses on different regions. As J.C. Shairp points out in *The Treatment of Nature in Sangam Literature*, "Nature is always man's spirit in manifold and mysterious ways, to elevate him with its vastness and sublimity, to gladden him with its beauty, to depress him with its bleakness and to restore him with its calm" (28). The literary conventions of the Sangam Age are seen not only in gracious blending of human passions with the beauties of nature but also in the division of the sentiments of love in accordance with the different regions and assigning them to particular seasons and hours. When the setting of the novels in Tamil literature are taken into consideration, it is undoubtedly based on one of the five regions – the *kurunji* or the mountain region, the *mullai* or the forest or pastoral tract, the *marutham* or the agricultural region, the *neytal* or the coastal region and the *palai* or the arid desert tract. The world of Rajanarayanan is an agricultural region so the people in his works are associated with works related to agriculture.

The novels of Rajanarayanan promulgate the fact that man has to consider nature as a teacher in order to learn a lot from the boundless, mysterious repository of information for his own well-being. His novels constantly echo the fact that modern man has alienated from nature and has also tried every means to exploit nature and its beings. After losing all the water bodies and trees to the unquenchable rapacity of human beings who have taken complete control over all the natural resources, it is pathetic to see birds taking shelter and resting in the shady twigs and plants. Hence his novels also advocate the significance of the preservation of nature.

Rajanarayanan's works provide us with a clear picture of the dependence of man on nature and man's attempts to establish a close affinity with it and the various ordeals of man's struggles against nature for his survival. Though man struggles hard to combat and win nature, he is aware of the impossibilities and hence surrenders himself to its powers. Nature to Rajanarayanan is not something that is hostile or inimical to mankind but is always a benevolent force and teacher who teaches the ethics of life.

A close analysis of Rajanarayanan's novels reveals that nature is copious or dense in his writings. As Prof. Panchangam rightly says in *Iyarkai Ezhuthuthalum Ki.Rajanarayananum*, nature writing is something beyond the amalgamation of aesthetics in human passions and is considered a practical technique or strategy to chisel human culture through the representation of the harmonious relationship between man and nature. Nature writing does not mean simply writing about nature or admiring nature with the imaginative faculty of human mind or using fictive and flowery language to adore the magnificence of nature but it is a record of an acute observation of the various activities of nature and their influence on human life in different aspects. It is not about the veneration or admiration of the different aspects of nature but it is a quest for the philosophical vision of life. Though it is claimed that man has gone far away from nature, it is ludicrous to say that man exists outside the realm of nature. Man cannot feel the presence of nature through the medium of language however beautifully it is presented to him. The bond between man and the five elements of nature is so deep, passionate and intertwined that man cannot unfetter from the influences of nature. Moreover, nature remains an eternal mystery and everlasting beauty to the eyes of human beings. The profound relationship between man and the landscape is developed practically in all of Rajanaryanan's works.

The works of Rajanarayanan with the intrinsic and the extrinsic aspects of life set forth the inextricably intertwined truths of nature and humanity. Both man and nature have a place in his works, but the author lays great emphasis on man. Nature is the stage on which man enacts his role. He has acutely and minutely observed and recorded his appreciation of nature in his works and the various effects it in an agricultural community. In his attempts to portray an agricultural community and the efforts of the individuals to form such a community in his world of creation, he records the fusion or blend of those people with every aspect of nature with great accuracy and admiration.

Though man is the focal point in the novels of Rajanarayanan and nature is made subservient to the human theme, there is effective as well as abundant use of nature and the writer has no reserve in the treatment of the natural world of his Karisal region with all its wonders and ghastly things. Unlike the poets of the Sangam Literature or the Romantic poet William Wordsworth, Rajanarayanan does not prostrate at the beauty and wonder of nature; he even does not get infused with the divine quality of nature and fallen into a trance like condition. Rather his curiosity to observe nature accurately and minutely gets reinforced and every second of his journey towards nature and the awe-inspiring elements of it are recorded in his writings with artistic beauty and realism. His admiration for nature is thus quoted: "I took shelter in school not to study but to avoid getting drenched in rain. After taking shelter in the school, my attention was completely captured by the rain not by the teaching" (Meera 12). It is very evident from these words that he is so fond of nature that he could make the readers visualize and get impressed with every aspect of nature. His description of the flora and fauna of his region proves his intimate knowledge and keen observation of their way of life.

His first novel *Gopalla Kiramam* deals with the travails and endurance of an agricultural community against nature as well as threats of bandits. *Gopalla Kiramam* tells the history of the settlement of Kammavars, a migrated Telugu speaking community from Andhra Pradesh in the plains of the southern parts of Tamil Nadu. The reign of the Muslim Kings in Andhra Pradesh before the arrival of the British in India had made many families suffer a lot. One such family, the Kottayars had to leave their homeland in fear of a Muslim king who had a great interest in keeping Chenna Devi, a beautiful girl of the Kottaiyar's family as one of his mistresses. This novel provides a detailed picture of the various hardships faced by the community during their journey towards the southern part of Tamil Nadu. It also pictures how the migrated community fought against nature in order to make a wild cacti forest into an arable land and a place of their living. As the title suggests, the whole novel revolves around the village Gopallapuram and its inhabitants who all gather at a place for the trial of a bandit who murders a pregnant woman for her ear rings. The innocent pregnant woman, after quarrelling with her husband, comes to a spring to quench her thirst after walking down miles on the Mangamma road is murdered by the bandit. Though this seems to be the main plot of the novel, the author's mastery lies in the depiction of the famine brought by the locusts in the village, the migrated community's struggle in the cacti forest with weeds and other insects that pose a great threat to their farming land and the impact of East India Company on the rural folks.

Place and time are the primary elements of nature to man, according to the greatest Grammarian Tholkkappiar. These two elements are indispensable not only to common man but also to creators who create stories about man. It is impossible to create a story without showing when and where an event takes place. These two elements are vital to the readers too in order to have a better understanding of the plot. Rajanarayanan has given prominence to these two elements. His affinity with the place is illustrated in the following lines:

I love my land and people immensely. This is the land where I was born. This is the land on which I crawled, fell down, and played with great delight. I was delighted to smear the soil on my head and the heads my friends. I was beaten up by my parents many times for having tasted this black soil. I have never been satiated with the soil even now. (*Katturaigal* 165)

The way Rajanarayanan celebrates the beauty of Karisal soil is unique and unparalleled in Tamil literature. To the people of the Karisal region, their land or soil is the panacea or remedy to all their illness. When people suffer from stomach pain or their cattle afflicted with diseases, it is believed that eating a pinch of soil or smearing the soil on their foreheads is the best medicine to get rid of the problems. The man who considers his sheep the only world is thus introduced:

Ramakkonar suffered from severe stomach pain while herding his sheep. Turning at the direction of Thiruchendur, he raised his hands above his head all of a sudden and loudly uttered 'Muruga! Muruga!' keeping his eyes closed. Then he prostrated in worship in the remained still in the position for some time. After a few minutes he got up and put a pinch of soil into his mouth and head and smeared a little on his forehead and wiped off his eyes with his towel tied on his waist. His stomach ache would disappear without any symptom after a while. Then he would cry later. But this time it's not out of agony but out of ecstasy. (*Kathaigal* 457)

There is a custom prevailing even today among the rustic community that old people in death bed are given a few drops of milk or water mixed with the soil of their land. After the consumption of this, they die. There are many such incidents in the stories of Rajanarayanan. Annarappa Kounder's soul got departed from his body only after he was fed with a spoon of water mixed with the black soil taken from his land which he was his life and soul. This is an illustration of the affinity that a farmer in the Karisal region has with his land. To the people living in rural areas, especially to a farming community, the land is everything to them. Land is the main source of living. When Mangaiathaar Ammal and her ancestors arrived in Karisal region, they chose a thick cacti forest as their place of settlement. It was she who pointed out the south and ordered the immigrants to weed out the thicket of spurges and make it a grazing ground for the cattle.

Agricultural community takes great pride in saying that their life is superior to the peripatetic life of the hunting and shepherding community as they need not wander from one place to another for their survival. Land and cattle are the primary wealth of the agricultural community. The bondage between man and land, man and animals in a farming community surpasses all other relationships in the world. Due to industrialization, urbanization, economic instability, globalization, political turmoil and ethnic crisis in the technological era, rural farmers have to leave their homelands and migrate to other areas in search of their livelihood.

When they go to other places leaving their homeland and cattle, their memories are always on their homeland and cattle. The realistic picture of the lamentation of people over the loss of land and cattle is recorded in *Gopalla Kiramam*. When Mangaiathaar and her ancestors had fled away from their homeland, their memories were haunted by their land and cattle. It was distressing to leave them. Their feeling of distress is described thus: "Their hearts pined for their home soil and the people they had left behind. They would speak fondly about the cattle: the cows, the calves ... every single living thing back home" (*GKM* 55)

Since the origin of mankind on this earth, nature remains a mysterious force to man. Even a handful of soil contains millions and millions of organisms which are unseen by man with his naked eyes. He is astonished to see the innumerable varieties of plants grown in the soil and the chemical reactions happening in the soil day after day. The custom of tasting the soil of Mother earth is prevalent not only in Karisal region but is prevalent in all the agricultural societies. This custom in Karisal society is shown by Rajanarayanan to his readers through a character called Mannuthinni Rangaiyya Nayakkar.

Mannuthinni Rangaiyya Nayakkar was named so not because of his habit of eating soil as some children do due to malnourishment but because of his expertise in assessing the quality and strength of soil. The entire community sought his help when they wanted to buy a piece of land from somebody. Just by putting a pinch of soil into his mouth, he could assess the suitability of land for the kind of crops grown in it. Even he could say whether the land was fertile or infertile. There is nothing to feel amazed by the uniqueness of Mannuthinni; it is because that every farmer in the land is endowed with such a quality.

The reverence that people in agricultural societies have for their land is exemplified in many instances in *Gopalla Kiramam*. During those days, before the arrival of suction pumps in the Karisal villages, people had to rely on rain. The land that is tilled after the first showers in summer is called 'ezhupidippu'. This makes it easier, during the rains, for the water to enter the ground and wash away the weeds. Using one plough to till the land before the next rain was a difficult job for them as they could not till the land completely before the start of next shower. Akkaiyya had thought of designing a pair of ploughs, lighter in weight and capable of digging the ground deeper. His efforts were finally paid off. This is described by the author thus: "The ploughs no longer ran into each other at every turn. They gripped tight as they tilled. The soil turned over on either side like ripples. Mother Earth bowed her head and paid respect to the farmer's effort" (*GKM* 48). When the mother Earth, the great supporter of mankind was trampled by the White officials and the black assistants, the Karisal farmers considered their deed a sin and perhaps reproached them saying thus: "it is not right to allow them to put their feet heavily on our Earth for no reason" (*GKM* 148). This is a typical scene of the celebration of the land which is their prime source of livelihood and of the intimacy the Karisal people had on their land.

The bond between human and non-human beings especially cows in the agrarian society such as Karisal is reinforced by the author in the description of saving the life of a pregnant cow that is caught in a slushy pond. In order to save the life of the cow, the whole village join hands together and put their concerted effort to bring up the cow from the slushy pond. On seeing the cow's stomach, it was recognized by the villagers that it was pregnant and it might deliver a calf in a day or two. The news of the cow reached the entire village and everybody gathered around the pond to witness how it could be rescued. Four or five young men of the village went into the pond to drag the cow ashore; it was a great challenge for them as the cow seemed to have wandered and grazed all alone without the sight and touch of human beings since birth. The young men had entered the slush to drag the cow out. They threaded the cow's nostrils with wild plants, which they twined. The grandmother sitting on the bank warned the men that the cow could not be tamed with the nose rope as it was a wild one and asked them to clinch the rope to the end of the nostrils. The cow bellowed loudly when the nostrils were pierced. It splashed the slush on the crowd. The young men drew the rope through the holes and dragged the cow to the bank. The scene of dragging the cow is described thus: "It was almost as if an army of forty or fifty ants had reamed through a worm and were dragging it off" (*GKM* 85). Though there is selfishness in the villagers' act of rescuing the cow, it also signifies their love for the animal. This is manifested clearly when Mangaiathaar Ammal tells Govindappa the reason for naming their village: "Mahalakshmi came to us along with that cow. Since then we have had plenty of cows. We even named our village Gopalla because of these cows" (*GKM* 86).

The efforts of Rajanarayanan in awakening eco-consciousness in people through his writings deserve a thorough examination. There are many instances in *Gopalla Kiramam* which substantiates the author's efforts displaying the man-nature relationship. When the migrants reached the Gopalla village after many days of arduous journey, the place where they finally settled, was once upon a time a thicket, fully surrounded by wild, thorny shrubs and cactus plants. They had battled hard to destroy the forest in order to make the land suitable for cultivation. With the instruments they possessed, they struggled a lot to cut the thorny bushes down. So some migrants suggested an idea to destroy the forest completely by fire but the idea was not advocated by everyone because most of them had the same feeling that it was easy to destroy it but realized the difficulties to create one when needed. After realising that their attempts of making an arable land would be futile if they kept on cutting down the bushes, they decided to destroy it by fire. Before it was done, they looked for an auspicious day. They really worried about the consequences of destroying nature. Just moments before they set ablaze the forest, an old grandmother in a loud voice said, "Oh' the angels of the forest, woodland deities, you must protect us from the repercussions for the deadly act of ours" (*GKM* 87). To make atonement for the destruction caused by the villagers to nature, the entire village decided that each of the families would have to plant a tree in remembrance. Every tree along the bank had been planted by the families of that village and had been reared with care for generations and they stood majestic as a dense forest.

The cacti forest chosen by the immigrants as their place of settlement had never experienced the smell of human beings before. Having understood the difficulties of struggling against nature such as poisonous insects, wild animals and venomous snakes, just like the ancient men tamed nature without being hostile towards it, the immigrants did follow the same approach. The congeniality and dependence of nature by the rural community is manifested in the novel when the author describes the various things that nature had given to the migrants during their initial days of their struggle towards clearing the cacti forest into an arable land. The forest had given them a lot of palm fruits, cucumbers, cacti fruits and tomatoes. Further, they had found plenty of sweet-smelling tapioca roots, edible plants and leaves and a lot of eggs of different kinds of birds. Some had eaten aloe plants after removing the outer layer and rinsing well with water to get rid of its bitterness. People who live in close communion are aware of the fact that a plant like aloe is the panacea for all kinds of diseases. The water in the grove tasted like nectar. It even had the capacity to allay hunger and provided them with vigour and energy. They hunted birds and animals for their food. There were bountiful beehives everywhere in the forest. They took bowls and bowls of fresh honey. They had their roasted meat mixed with honey. For future use or rainy season, they even saved some meat mixed with salt.

Rajanarayanan not only shows the benign force of nature but also the ruthlessness of it through a famine caused by locusts. Towards the end of the novel, when Seeni Nayakkar and Engathci were indulging in a sensual game after their breakfast, they heard the loud screeching of their pet parrot in terror. They immediately came to the inner courtyard and were stunned to see hounds of insects buzzing around and covering the top of their favourite curry tree. Every leaf on the tree started to disappear. Very soon, the air was filled with alarming human cries. It was as if the entire village had become a beehive and locusts were the flies buzzing around it. People in the village were seen wailing, slapping their chests and mouths. Those guarding the fields rushed to chase the locusts away, hitting them with sticks. The villagers had never seen such big locusts in their lives before nor had they heard about them. There were locusts on the plants in the fields too. Not a single plant was visible, only a sea of locusts. "The forest air was filled with their neruk neruk hum" (GKM 143). The plants had grown tall and thick. That year's growth was sumptuous across the village. They had been planning to start the harvest the next day when the catastrophe happened. Farmers were not able to bear the misfortune when their hard labour was ravaged by the locusts. Every field of the farmers in the village was decimated by the locusts.

Another important feature in the depiction of nature or the non-human world is Time. Time is a mysterious controlling force of mankind. As there are different periods of Time such as present, past and future, there are different times of a day such as dawn, dusk, twilight and night. If *Gopalla Kiramam* describes the various activities of birds and animals happening at dawn such as the returning of cats to their homes slowly crawling back into their shells and the racing of owls to their roosts and the hurrying of bandicoots into their burrows and the race for survival at the banks of rivers and lakes, *Gopallapurathu Makkal* begins with the description of activities happening in the evening.

As the title of the novel indicates, it focuses much on the people of Gopalla Village rather than nature. Rajanarayanan received the prestigious literary award Sahitya Academy Award for this novel. It is a sequel to *Gopalla Kiramam* and the plot is based on the historical events such as the Indian independence movement and the reactions of the villagers especially the Karisal villagers against East India Company and the strong feelings of the farmers who protested against the British rule in India.

The uniqueness of this work of Rajanarayanan lies in the fact that this novel is perceived by many as a compilation of various events rather than a fiction. Besides focusing on the rural community's reaction towards struggle for independence from the

British, this novel also throws light on the dawn of civilization or modernization in Karisal village and the various impacts it makes on the lives of common people. The effects of new things such as tea powder, matchbox, torch light and kerosene lamps are realistically portrayed by the author. Rajanarayanan's views on English medium schools in small towns and the rules and regulations drawn by the East India Company are highlighted with wit and sarcasm. The last part of the novel focuses on the Indian independence struggle and the fortitude of the people who participated in the struggle with great artistic ability.

Though *Gopallapurathu Makkal* lays emphasis on the portrayal of the idiosyncrasies of individual characters, there are many descriptions of nature and the portrayal of the minute observations of the behaviour of animals especially cows that deserve special attention. The harmonious relationship between man and animals in the rural world is depicted in the liveliest manner. Along with other human characters, the wild cow 'Kaari' that comes to the village plays a very significant role in the novel. The eco-consciousness of the rural folks and the interconnectedness between human and non-human beings are exemplified in this novel too.

Cows are considered as an integral part of the agricultural community; without cows, the lives of the farmers would be difficult. The love and reverence shown by people towards cows is depicted through a cow called Sembarai which is personified. During the harvest season, it is the custom of the village poet 'Kavirayar' to come to the field early in the morning and to sing in praise of god, cows and farmers. Listening to his songs, the field works are carried out by the farmers. When god created various living organisms in the world, he sent each organism with a purpose to carry out certain tasks. When he sent the cows, he told them that it should plough the earth and drag the ploughs. They should carry the loads. They should be helpful to mankind. They should also provide milk to the infants and save them from dying of hunger without milk. After listening to the commands of the god, they stood in silence without nodding their heads as a sign of approval. Looking at the cows, god asked them to express what was in their minds. The thoughts of the cows were expressed by the author in the most realistic way thus:

Without roping me in the shed the whole day, I should be allowed to wander for a few hours.

My progenitors and I should not be tortured.

During green season, we should be fed with grass at least once a day.

During the harvest of millet, our mouths should not be strapped.

Yearly once, we should be treated with respect by offering pongal to us in our shed and our horns be smeared with yellow powder and kumkum. (*GKM* 162)

After listening to the demands of the cows, human beings acceded to them. This episode evinces how sympathetic and understandable rural community is towards animals. People in rural areas have a thorough understanding of nature and its beings and they treat every organism living in the earth with respect. They are aware of the fact that they are no way superior to other creatures in this world. The description of the beauty of cows indicates that the rural community is basically egalitarian in nature.

It is the custom of the village to offer cows to the village temple as a sign of gratitude to god who provides them immense wealth. As it is a miracle to see human beings with great beauty, it is a great wonder to see a calf born with alluring beauty. When such a bull calf is born, the villagers do not think of rearing it and keeping it for their own purpose. As soon as the calf stops drinking milk and starts chewing hay, it is left in the village's 'Perumal temple on an auspicious day with great celebration. After offering pongal to the bull calf and making a sign of 'naamam' on its back with a red hot iron rod, it is left free. The mark of 'naamam' may indicate to the onlookers that is a temple cow. Such a bull has its liberty and it cannot be tortured or beaten up by anyone in the village even if it eats the crops grown in the fields of the farmers.

Such independently grazed calf becomes a young bull and comes to the village's cow sheds and makes the other young cows pregnant. It is only for this purpose that the villagers bear all the destructions caused by the beautiful bull. This also paves way for the cows to give birth to high breed calves. There are many oral stories about such temple bulls in the Karisal village. Once a temple calf grows into a young bull, it feels attached with the village only for three to four years. After that, it becomes hostile towards the villagers and breaks its relationship with people and instils a kind of fear in the minds of people. The way the bull shakes its head with its sharp horns may seem to be inviting men for a fight.

The novel also records the arrival of 'Kaari,' a wild bull in the Karisal village. The way the description of its arrival clearly shows that Rajanarayanan is a not only great story teller but also a man with profound knowledge about the behaviour of animals. No other writer has the ability to narrate the incident of the arrival of Kaari in the most fascinating way as Rajanarayanan does. One day Nandhagoban went to the low hills to get some leaves. On seeing a beautiful, young and grey-coloured bull in the midst of the forest, he was joyous and astonished by the appearance of it. He was stunned to see such a wild and beautiful bull. The bull seemed to have severed its relationship with a village and started living in the forest. Its sharp horns and hump were covered with mud as it had dug the ground. Nandhagoba Nayakkar looked at it sternly and decided to take his flock the next day to the low hills with the intention and desire of having such a bull in his flock.

Attracted by the smell of one of the cows, one day Kaari came to Nandhagoban's flock when his cows were grazing the field in the low hills. On seeing the approach of Kaari at a distance, young boys climbed up the trees and Nandhagoban climbed up a high rock. Breaking all the well grown plants and saplings, he came in search of the cows. The rest of the scene is described thus: "Raising its head a little high as if it were to sneeze, the bull neared the cow. The other cows were grazing the field without showing any concern about the approach of the bull. 'Only human beings do not have any other work, said Nandhagoban to himself'" (*GKM* 186).

The bull spent the whole day with the cow in Nandagoban's flock. There was a sense of fear in his mind that the bull would take away his cow to the forest along with it. When the time arrived to take the flock back to the pen, Kaari accompanied the cow to some distance and then it stopped.

The cow that mated with Kaari had given birth to a beautiful calf bull that resembled its father. Everybody in Nandhagoban's house felt much elated on seeing the beauty of the baby Kaari. As usual when it grew up, it was offered to the village temple. Even after it was left free, it used to come to his shed in the evening. The custom prevailed in the village did not allow them to tie it back in the shed so they sent it out. However the children in Nandhagoban's house used to offer something to it secretly.

The love and affection shown by the villagers to such cows like Kaari was not shown even to fellow human beings. This is exemplified by Rajanarayanan through the reaction of Lakshmanna when his servant came to him to complain about the ravage caused by the temple cow in his millet field. In a fit of fury, he left for the field but came home smilingly. "Hey fool, after its grazing, the rest is only ours, he said" (GKM 188). The words of Lakshmanna were unbearable to the servant Kazhuvan. "Only one eighth of the total yield is given to him though he is the one who ploughs the land, sows the seeds and waters them day and night and struggles a lot in the field" (GKM 189).

Through the description of the fierce battle between the two bulls Kaari and Pullai, the author draws an analogy between human beings and cows. Cows have all the traits of human beings and the same kind of feeling of jealousy and envy. The smell of the cows in Gopalla village had attracted the neighbouring village temple bull Pullai. The red soil on its body and chisel like horns and the marks on its body due to the falling of cacti milk indicated that it could have come from the neighbouring village. The very appearance of Pullai from the neighbouring village enraged the local temple bull Kaari and it approached towards Pullai. When the two bulls encountered face to face, they rubbed the ground with their hoofs and started fighting each other fiercely. They fought for a long time. The spectators were not able to guess who would win the fight. The sharp pointed horns of Pullai tore the face and body of Kaari and blood oozed out. Kaari was determined not to allow Pullai into its territory. Just like man struggles to protect his land, animals too have the same instinct of protecting their lands.

The non-human world of Rajanarayanan also pictures some bizarre events which the readers would have never come across before. One such event in *Gopallapurathu Makkal* is the scene of a baby goat sucking the udder of a cow. The exploitation of Nature by human beings is also presented in the novel. When a cow gives birth to a dead calf, man knows it is not possible to milk from the cow, so he employs a clever trick to make a new born calf born to another cow which is dead at the time of delivery. This is called 'thazhaiyarathu'. It is not an easy deed to unite a new born calf with another cow that has lost its young one as cow has a great power of sniffing. It is not possible to make a cow feed a motherless calf even in pitch dark. After sniffing, it will kick the calf away.

In another instance, the author focuses on providing water to the cows in the most dramatic way. As we find human beings with different individualistic traits, cows are also different in nature and have many individualistic traits as humans have. For example, some cows drink water only mixed with salt. Some cows prefer to have water mixed with vinegar. Some prefer to have bran; some prefer to have oil cake along with milk extracted from cotton seeds. Some even like to have millet rice. When the author talks about the way cows understand the feelings of human beings, it shows the rural community's strong relationship with animals especially cows.

Cows are very astute animals. They understand human emotions like anger and impatience somehow. Truly, they never succumb to such human emotions. When his mother was alive she used to say, 'Nagaiyya, when you feed the cows with hay, pat them on their backs and caress them. You provide them water with love and affection. Never express your anger at the time of feeding.

(*Kathaigal* 217)

The next novel *Andaman Nayakkar* highlights the ordeals of the freedom fighters in Andaman prison and the callous attitude of the bureaucrats towards farmers in the independent India. This work is a tribute to the agricultural labourers who lost their lives in the protest against the ruthlessness of the revenue officials who seized the properties of the rustics for not having paid the bank loans and the revised land taxes at the time of severe famine and drought. This novel is a realistic portrayal of a traditional rural village which focuses on the torments of an innocent peasant in the hands of the British police in Andaman Jail during the pre-independence period and the pain inflicted by the unsympathetic or apathetic attitude of politicians, local police and the corrupt bureaucrats who constitute the Indian society in the post independent India. The novel testifies the predicament of the peasants in an agricultural society. This novel clearly exposes the miserable plight of the poor peasants and other ordinary labourers who form a major part of the rural society. Although the main focus of the novel is the expression of anguish and agony of a rural farm labourer named Andaman Nayakkar in a remote village, through this character the author skilfully exposes the endurance, loyalty, selflessness, humanity and other traits that are native to every denizens in the rural community. This novel is a kind of political satire that exposes the injustice meted out to innocent rural folks who are torn asunder between traditionalism and modernity. The novelist's skill in exposing the existence of colonialism in one form or the other is evident throughout the novel. The importance of work for the villagers and the portrayal of humble but articulate community representatives of the Karisal region exemplify the positives of village life.

The rural community as a unified, harmonious network of individuals is given more prominence in *Andaman Nayakkar* and is portrayed with a mixture of depression and gloom. There are many incidents in the novel that records the loss of an ancient rural tradition or the impact of westernization in rural society, the collective activities of the villagers in the rally against the tax levied upon lands illustrate the survival of many other old and enduring rural customs such as integrity, unity and solidarity in times of crises. Though this novel depicts hardships encountered by farmers in rural societies, rustic customs and strong determination and integrity of rural folks, the main theme is betrayal. While there is a strong connection between Gopalla Kiramam and Gopallapurathu Makkal, it may be noted that Andaman Nayakkar is completely divergent from the other two.

However benign nature is to mankind, the farmers in the Karisal region have to struggle against weeds which are considered their worst enemies. Rajanarayanan is of the opinion that weeds are like green fire which has the potential to devastate the entire field. Weeds have the ability to grow faster than crops and can absorb water and nutrients quickly. Only crops are afflicted by diseases and insects; weeds are not.

Pinchugal is a novella that centres on the life of a Karisal boy named Venkatesh. The world of children in Karisal region is reflected through this work by Rajanarayanan. Rajanarayanan makes an attempt to show how the life of children in Karisal region is interwoven with nature.The stage between the birth of a child and up till the age of twelve is called the childhood stage. There are amazing changes happening in the growth of children during this stage. As there is a gradual growth in the physique of the children, there is also a gradual development in their minds. This mental change happens continually as a process based on their experiences in life and the people around them. Thus it is said the development of a child happens due to the experiences of life. There is no limit to the mischief of children during this stage. The naughtiness of a child at this state or stage is beautifully portrayed in *Pinchugal.* A novel written by Tolstoy about his childhood days has greatly influenced Rajanarayanan to write this novel. Further, Rajanarayanan won the 'best literary thought' award for this novel in the year 1978. In this novel, Rajanarayanan wonderfully pictures the heart and mind of a child; especially his own self through the characters Venkatesh, Ashok and Senthilnathan. He also takes the readers to their own childhood reminiscences and evokes a kind of nostalgia. The children portrayed in this novel are known for their love for Nature, ingeniousness and mischief.

The psychological development of a child is based on the place, society and the milieu in which it lives. The social milieu around which a child lives has a great impact on its behaviour. This novel is a compilation of the various incidents that happen in a village. Various characters such as Venkatesh, Senthilnathan and Ashok are fond of nature because of their environment in which they live. As these boys live in close communion with nature and breathe in everything that is natural, they show a lot of love for nature and its beings. Besides showing a great love and affection for nature, they enjoy every minute of their life in the wondrous environment surrounded by plants and trees. The chief character Venkatesh is fond of birds. He learns the unique traits of the different kinds of birds from Thiruvethi Nayakkar. His curiosity to know about the birds is evident from the way he asks questions about the birds.

One day Thiruvethi Nayakkar observes Venkatesh climbing down the top of a tree. He goes near him and asks affectionately the reason for his climbing the tree. Venkatesh says immediately,

I need the egg of a crow

Why do you need the egg of a crow? asks Thiruvethi.

Along with the egg of a crow I need the egg of a cuckoo as well. Is it true uncle that a cuckoo lays its egg in the nest of a crow? asks Venkatesh. (*Pinchugal* 27)

With lot of affection, Thiruvethi Nayakkar caresses the arm of Venkatesh. The next day Venkatesh shows him the eggs of the birds he has saved. On seeing them, Thiruvethi behaves like a child and looks at the different colours, sizes of the birds' eggs with amazement. This is how the relationship between Thiruvethi Nayakkar and Venkatesh gets strengthened. The ability to admire the beauty of Nature is inherent in Venkatesh.

Another day, a flock of mynah are singing and bathing happily in a long canal. Watching this from a little distance, Venkatesh is quite surprised to see them drying their feathers soon after bathing and he just thinks of that scene as if they are all getting ready for a wedding ceremony. Again, on another day, when he is playing under a tree, he finds a young mynah falling down when its mother is teaching it to fly. Immediately, he picks the mynah from the ground and carries it to his friend's house and asks his sister Manga to cut off its feather. After a few days, we find the mynah speaking the human language which is a surprise to everyone. This is how the protagonist's love for mynahs begins.

Venkatesh who has been suffering from chicken pox for many days, is met by his friends Ashok and Senthil. At that time, Senthil puts his hands into his pocket and takes out a small marble sized egg and hands it over to his friend Venkatesh. Ashok asks him curiously what it is. Senthil asks him to close his hands tightly and they wonder whether it is a hen's egg. They are not able to believe it because very rarely a hen lays such an egg.

During the meeting, Ashok describes his journey to the nearby town Kovilpatti. In his journey, he happens to see a man selling medicine for scorpion bite. The seller is surrounded by onlookers. To his surprise he has neither seen such a big scorpion nor heard of such a big one.

You won't believe me, it is such a huge scorpion. It is about 30 cm long and 15 cm width. Legs are like our fingers. After the legs there is a sharp pointed, red colour sting. Oh god, I get goose bumps even I think of that now exclaims Senthil. And he further says that it is not called as scorpion it is a giant spider. (*Pinchugal* 42)

Senthil immediately recollects the day he has seen the preserved feathers of the dead peacocks displayed by the Kuravas in Kovilpatti. It is always pleasant to look at the beauty of the muster of peacocks. After a great difficulty, Venkatesh could bring two peacock's eggs and try to hatch it along with the hens' eggs. But his attempts to hatch the eggs are prevented by his parents. This has caused a feeling of disappointment to him. He decides to establish a farm for peacocks once he grows up. This is how the children of the Karisal region develop interest in animals and birds as they live in harmony with it. On seeing the different coloured birds, different shapes of their eggs etc, they develop a strong interest in them.

Children are usually endowed with lots of talent. Those children who are cleverer than the children of their age group are seen with lot of energy and briskness. These children sometimes outwit the elders with their ability to question. The kinds of question the clever children ask indicate their cognitive, learning and personality traits. One day Venkatesh requests Thiruvethi Nayakkar to aim at a mynah on a tree with the help of his catapult. Thiruvethi Nayakkar decides not to kill it and says that it is not good to kill a bird which is beneficial to mankind. Immediately Venkatesh questions him then why does he (Thiruvethi Nayakkar) kill a quail and eat its meat as if the birds destroy their grains? Thiruvethi is stunned by the brilliant question of the boy and appreciates him.

There are many mischievous games played in the childhood stage. Every game played by children indicates their naughtiness. One day when Venkatesh comes out of his friend's house Senthil, he happens to see children playing the game of bride and bridegroom. On seeing this game he is reminded of the various games he played during his childhood days. Once the trios, Senthil, Ashok and Venkatesh go to a railway station to quench their thirst. As usual, when they reach a station, they see a goods train passing them. They count the number of coaches individually; again there is variation in their counting.

After quenching their thirst in the railway station, they come to the nearby Amman temple and take rest under a tree. There are many flowers bloom in the ground. These flowers are grey in colour and they look beautiful. There are many worms under the flower and children catch those worms and kill them for their happiness. This is one of the common sports of the children in the region. Even at a tender age, he along with the children of his age group adopt very strategies to catch birds like quail, mynah etc.

While describing the world of birds and animals, the author does not just stop with the portrayal of external things that he observes. Perhaps, he goes one step further and attempts to present the inner state of mind of animals and birds also. This is vivid when he expresses the inner feelings of birds and animals when they come to know about the departure of Venkatesh to the town for his higher studies. The description goes like this: "It is such a happy news for them. The young ones of all the birds will be safe henceforth. The birds returning to the nests may return happily once they come to know of his departure" (*Pinchugal* 64)

On one hand, his departure may be a happy news to all the birds; on the other hand, the cat which is reared in the house of Venkatesh will desperately look for him as there is no one to provide her the tasty meat of rabbit, birds and white rats. The dog 'Sivappi' will cry in search of its master, Venkatesh. Thus the personality of an individual is determined by the society in which he lives. As the children of the Karisal village live one with nature, their interests, hobbies and sports are associated with the things around them. Their knowledge about the world of animals, birds and plants is phenomenal.

Pinchugal exemplifies Rajanarayan's world of animals, plants and birds. In addition to expressing his knowledge of the natural world, this novel illustrates his love and admiration of the natural world. Rustic life is so interwoven with nature. The plants, animals and birds in the region live along with human beings. They are dependent on each other for their survival. They cannot be separated. The interdependency of these beings astonishes the readers. The characters like Venkatesh, Ashok, Senthivel, Thiruvethi Nayakkar etc and the incidents that revolve around them represent the natural world and the various cultural aspects of rustic life. The description of the qualities of birds and animals and their behaviour shows the realm of nature which is unknown to many of us. The minute details that the author records in this novel like the various sounds made by the birds clearly illustrate the author's love for the natural world. Similarly when the author describes the bathing of mynahs in the long stretch of rivulet or stream, it shows how he enjoys not only experiencing himself but also letting the world know that many of us even cannot think of such scenes.

The life of people living in the rural areas is more interesting than that of the life of people in the urban areas. Particularly the life of children in the rural areas is more realistic and it deserves a lot of attention. Rajanarayanan diverts his attention from portraying the life of the adults to the life of the children in his region. The naughtiness of children and the expression of their exuberance while playing with natural things, the realistic expression of their inner feelings while observing the behaviour of flora and fauna are brought out by the author in the most interesting and natural manner.

It is repeatedly told by many critics that one of the most unique qualities of Rajanarayanan is his ability to picture or portray things or persons that he sees in the realistic way as they are. While describing the characters with dishevelled hair or stained teeth or the muddy covered hands of the children while playing in the soil, the author presents them without changing the colour or the aroma of the land. This could be the reason for his success as a regional novelist. Not only the people, but also the images, similes that he makes use in his novels are mixed with the soil of his region.

There is a common weakness to man. The weakness is nothing but hearing of stories. When we look at children playing in the rural areas, many a time we find a child surrounded by many and the one sitting in the middle narrates a story. It is noted that there is no room for arguments or interferences when the story is narrated. There will be unexpected references to natural things or elements. The children around the story teller listen to the story with absolute silence and interest. It will be interesting even to the onlookers. This is the technique employed by Rajanarayanan in his stories.

As stated before this novel gains prominence in Tamil Children's Literature as it focuses on the inner feelings of children who live in harmonious relationship with nature. After reading this novel, there is no doubt that not only children but also adults observe nature and its beings with intense passion and love. The lines of the great poet Bharati 'birds and crows are my community and the blue sea and the mountain are my clan' become true in the novel *Pinchugal*. The characters like Venkatesh, Ashok, Senthivel, and Thiruvethi Nayakkar find a permanent place in the history of Tamil Literature. When the protagonist of the novel Venkatesh leaves his village to pursue his studies, along with the cows, dogs and cats of his house, the readers too shed tears. The animalistic nature of human beings becomes vanished and the divine trait of love and affection sprouts when we live in close communion with nature.

One of the important traits of a naturalist like Rajanarayanan is the tendency to look at all things equally without showing any personal likes or dislikes. This way of looking at all creatures with equality is evident in this novel. For example, the character of Venkatesh is delineated in such a way that he looks at all the birds with the same curiosity and passion. It is more evident when he questions Thiruvedhi Nayakkar the reason for killing the birds like quail that does not harm humans.

The descriptions of the various kinds of birds provide ample proof of the author's profound knowledge of birds. The kind of relationship between human beings and birds in the agrarian society is of love and hate relationship. Moreover, the author says that the birds that feed on worms, insects and meat are the best friends to farmers as those birds would kill the insects or flies that cause destruction to the crops. Those birds should not be hunted. The author's enthusiasm in describing the various types of sparrow like – honey sparrow (Thane Chittu), flat sparrow (Thattai chittu), flower sparrow (poonchittu), silk sparrow (pattu chittu), thorn sparrow (mulchittu), yellow sparrow (manjal chittu), red sparrow (Senjittu) and black sparrow (karunchittu) shows clearly his knowledge about the birds and his keen observation of their behaviour like an ornithologist. When he talks about the extinction of such rare species of birds in the era of technology, it evinces his eco-consciousness.

The manner in which he describes the way the mynah's bathe in the rivers or lakes, exhibits the author's minute observation and passion for writing about birds' behaviour and the relationship between birds and water in the world of nature. In the descriptions of the manners and habits of the animals, the terrestrial, the amphibious, the arboreal, the aquatic and the aerial, the writer has evinced his power of minute observation and his love for nonhuman beings. The world of birds shown in *Pinchugal* is delightful and interesting. Not only the domestic animals like cows and ox but also wild animals like boar are dealt with in detail. The relationship between man and animals, man and birds in Indian civilization is associated with reverence to God. In Hindu mythology, there are many trees worshipped and the trees that provide haven for birds and animals are treated with reverence. Even animals like rat, pig, tortoise, horse, eagle and lion are also considered reincarnation of Gods in the Hindu mythology. When the author expresses the lamentation of a hunter who kills an eagle for a quill, he shows how eagles are worshipped as God in the Indian culture.

The primary reason for the enduring fascination for the novels of Hardy and Rajanarayanan is that both of them are true representatives of the faded life of simple, honest rustic way of living among cows, sheep, haystacks, hedgerows, and trees. The nostalgia of such a humble living among the trees, animals and birds is clearly seen in the setting of the background of their novels. If Hardy's novels depict the background of strong English oak trees, heaths, fern hills and green pastures, the novels of Rajanarayanan depict the background of the peasants living in a region which is known for its black soil, arid land with well grown cotton plants and wildly grown cacti forest. Though the background or the environment they represent is geographically divergent in nature, they together stand for the ideal rural life which is devoid of machines and motor cars. They together represent a world as Jonathan Bate in *The Song of the Earth* quotes "the spirit of Philip Larkin's England of shadows, meadows and lanes that are gone" (2).

The cynic of the present time may contend that the nostalgia for such a rural life is a cultural ailment. The works of Hardy and Rajanarayanan clearly suggests that our culture is in the grip of an epidemic. The yearning for a pristine environment which is characterized by untainted beauty seems to be a sign of sickness to the present generation known for scientific and industrial revolution. The proliferation of industries and the resultant social mobility have made people ignore and appreciate the beauty and wonder of nature. In such a scenario, the novels of Hardy and Rajanarayanan document rural customs of great antiquity and they together represent a world which has been on the brink of modernity. Standing on the Egdon Heath of Hardy, one can be deafened by the roaring of flying Air Force jets at the present time. On the other hand, in the Karisal region of Rajanarayanan, the fields once seen with maize, millet and cotton plants are now seen with tall buildings and huge chimneys. The loud explosions of the mountains and rocks at the distant places disrupt the tranquillity of fields. Instead of the buzzing of the bees and chirping of crickets, the honking of automobiles and speeding vehicles and the jarring noise made by industries are heard. On witnessing all the transformations in the rural environment which was once admired for its beauty and the harmony that existed between human beings and other nonhuman beings, the words of Jonathan Bate echo our ears that both the writers valued a world – for them it was vanishing and for us it had long vanished already – in which people lived in rhythm with nature.

A close analysis of the novels of Hardy and Rajanarayanan reveals that the writers have focused on the benevolent and malevolent forces of nature. Nature assumes the dual role of creator as well as destructor. The bio-centric attitude of the writers is expressed throughout their works by giving importance to nature that not only determines the fate of the characters but also shows that humans are neither better nor worse than other creatures and are simple and equal to every other creature in the world.

THREE
CONCLUSION

The two writers not only described the beauty and wonders of nature but also the undeniable power of nature over human beings. The perennial struggle of man against nature and the fate of mancontrolled by the supreme power of nature were thoroughly examined. Both the writers paid undue attention to various elements in nature such as flora and fauna and the impact caused by these elements in the lives of human beings. Like the deep ecologists, the two writers were aware of the seriousness of life to all living creatures in the universe and shared the same feeling of compassion and love towards birds and animals The portrayal of different places such as Weatherbury, Little Hintock, Egdon Heath in the novels of Hardy and the Karisal region which is known for its wild cacti forest and black soil in the novels of Rajanarayanan shows different kinds of nature. The cheerful, gentle and sublime aspects of nature as portrayed by the Romantics are replaced by a somber, gloomy and vicious nature in the later novels of Hardy. Similarly, in the novels of Rajanarayanan we could see the twin faces of nature – nature as a creator as well as destroyer of man's life.

Nature in the novels of these writers is portrayed not only as a mere backdrop in the sufferings of human drama but also a main character in their works. In the struggle for survival man has to always reckon with the forces of nature. There are at times when this would prove calamitous. In *Far from the Madding Crowd*, Gabriel Oak recognizes that the storm poses a distinct threat to Bathsheba's ricks. Nature appears as both creator and destroyer here, for it is ready to destroy the bountiful harvest that it has helped to create. The intervention of man in exigencies is a necessity. Aided by Bathsheba herself, Oak manages to safeguard the harvest, at the risk of his own life. His refusal to accept the possibility of disaster is in stark contrast with Troy's apathy at the approaching storm. If Gabriel had not acted quickly and courageously, Bathsheba's crops would have been ruined. Survival often depends on a prompt and sensible interpretation of nature's ways.

The correlation between landscape and character is exemplified in *Far from the Madding Crowd*. The meeting of Oak and Troy by Bathsheba in two different physical surroundings signify the two different personalities. Gabriel Oak is seen when he is occupied with the ewes in the lambing season which shows his dependability and his concern and care for tender life. On the other hand, Troy is met by her on a dark path which symbolizes gloominess.

In *The Return of the Native* and *The Woodlanders*, nature determines the outcomes of events. In fact, it directs the action. Egdon Heath controls the lives of its inhabitants in the same way as Old South's tree holds in its clutches the fate of several Hintock people. As soon as the tree is felled, John South dies and Giles loses his cottage. Giles also loses Grace and she consequently turns to Fitzpiers, while Giles has to look for somewhere to live. Eventually he has to live in a lonely, dilapidated hut and becomes seriously ill. This illness recurs with fatal results at the end of the summer. Although the tree has been cut down to save Old South's life, it brings nothing but misery. The implication here is the warning that a miscalculation of Nature may have devastating consequences as it does in *The Return of the Native*. Egdon Heath is described as the enemy of civilization and a place which could retard the dawn, sadden noon, anticipate the frowning of storms scarcely generated, and intensified the opacity of a moonless midnight to a cause of shaking and dread. There is no surprise that Eustacia feels everything is wrong on Egdon. It is a prison to her. She is at variance with her surroundings as she is alien and yearns to move out of it. As she fails to subdue herself to the hands of nature and is rebellious, the consequence she faces in her life is death. This novel is a clear illustration of how nature affects the life of man when he tries to sever his relationship with it. The outcome of many vital scenes in the novel shows the kind of relationship the characters have with the heath or with Nature. Hardy attempted to prove in this novel that man who tries to exploit Nature for his own sake perishes.

In *Tess of the d'Urbervilles* Hardy attempted to reflect the change in Tess's emotions through different nature imageries. As life in nature is born in spring season, Tess's story also begins in the same season of the year. Her life becomes gloomy or miserable during autumn as she is raped by Alec. Her life calms down again and her passion for Angel Clare starts developing with the advent of summer. Again, their marriage is symbolically doomed from the very beginning as it takes place during a cold New Year's Eve. The different seasons used by Hardy indicates the correlation between the plot and the happening of various events.

Unlike Wordsworth, Hardy did not conceive of nature as the projection of mysticism and divinity of a loving deity. Hardy saw beauty in nature but realized that such beauty only masked carnage and destruction, the chief features of the natural world. Hardy treated nature in his novels in a conspicuously unorthodox manner, portraying it as man's enemy and tormenter. Man is never helped or aided by nature but is thwarted and destroyed by her cruel and inexplicable tricks.

Though the twin faces of nature are found in the novels of Rajanarayanan, his novels promulgate the fact that man shoud consider nature as a teacher in order to learn from the boundless, repository of information for his own well being. However man in the works of Rajanarayanan struggle against nature for his livelihood, he does not treat it with contempt. Rather he is awestruck at the mysterious force of it. Nature is portrayed as an everlasting mystery and eternal beauty in the eyes of human beings. The intimate relationship between nature and man is exemplified in many places in *Gopallapuram*. For instances, the village Gopallapuram is named after the arrival of the cow Kaari. The collective decision made by the villagers to plant at least one tree in remembrance of each family after the destruction of the wild cacti forest is a clear indication of the eco-consciousness of the rustic community. The dependence of man on nature is exemplified when the author talks about the different varieties of food given by the Mother Earth during their attempt to clear away the wild forest for their settlement. At the same time, the misery caused by the immigrants to various birds and animals during their clearing of the cacti forest makes the villagers as well as the readers feel sympathetic towards animals and birds who become innocent victims to the exploitation of nature by men.

The description of the ravage caused by the locusts in the end of the novel *Gopallapuram* is again another symbolic representation to show that nature does not help only man because of his high order thinking ability. Here the author attempted to prove that nature is a neutral force that sees man and other beings alike.

In the novella *Pinchugal*, Rajanarayanan's knowledge about the various types of birds and their unique traits and the psychological state of the children towards nature in Karisal villages are portrayed through the protagonist Venkatesh. This work is a typical example to show how man's state of mind is shaped by the environment where he lives.

Of course, there are many differences in the portrayal of nature by both the writers; the thin line that unites them both is in presenting nature as a determining force of man's life. However the two writers differ in the treatment of nature, the converging view point is that man can survive, though not lead a happy life only when he maintains a perfect equilibrium with nature. The moment he tries to exploit nature for his own benefit, the repercussion is obviously suffering and death.

FOUR

REFERENCES

Primary Sources

Hardy, Thomas. *Far from the Madding Crowd*. London: Penguin Classics, 1978. Print. (Abbreviated as *FFMC*)

.... . *The Return of the Native*. New Delhi: UBS Publishers & Distributors Pvt. Ltd. 2012. Print. (Abbreviated as *TRTN*)

... . *The Woodlanders*. London: Wordsworth Classics, 2004. Print. (Abbreviated as *TWL*)

.... *Tess of d'Urbervilles*. London: Wordsworth Classics, 2000. Print. (Abbreviated as *TESS*)

Ki. Rajanarayanan. *Gopalla Kirama Makkal: A Trilogy*. Chennai: Kavya Publications, 2002. Print. (Abbreviated as *GKM)*

.... *Pinjugal*. Thanjavur: Annam Publications Pvt. Ltd. 2007. Print.

Secondary Sources

Abercrombie, Lascelles. *Thomas Hardy: A Critical Study*. London: Martin Secker, 1912. Print.

Alan D. Gilbert. The *Making of Post-Christian Britain: A History of the Secularization of Modern Society*. Addison-Wesley Longman Limited, 1980. Print.

Alexander Anne, *Thomas Hardy: The 'Dream-Country' of His Fiction*. London: Vision Press Ltd., 1976. Print.

Ambruster Karla and Kathleen R. Wallace, ed. *Beyond Nature Writing: Expanding the Boundaries of Ecocriticism*. Charlottesville and London: University Press of Virginia, 2001. Print.

Bailey James . *Thomas Hardy and the Cosmic Mind: A New Reading of the Dynasts*. University of North Carolina Press, 1956. Print.

Bassnett,Susan. *Comparative Literature: A Critical Introduction.* UK: Blackwell Publishers, 1993. Print.

Baral, K.C. *Sigmund Freud: A Study of His Theory of Art and Literature*. New Delhi: Sterling, 1995. Print.

Barry, Peter. *Beginning Theory: An Introduction to Literary and Cultural Theory.* 2nd ed. Manchester: Manchester UP, 2002. Print.

Bate, Jonathan. *Romantic Ecology: Wordsworth and the Environmental Tradition*. New York: Routledge, 1991. Print.

Bate, Jonathan. *The Song of the Earth.* London: Picador, 2000.

Bell, Michael. *Primitivism*. London: Methuen & Co. Ltd., 1972. Print.

Bentley P. Eleanor. *The English Regional Novel.* New York: Haskel House, 1966. Print.

Betty, J.H. *Rural Life in Wessex, 1500 -1900.* Gloucester: Allan Sutton Publishing Ltd. 1989. Print.

Blunden, Edmund. *Thomas Hardy*. 1942. London: Macmillan, 1962. Print.

Bratchell, D.F. *The Impact of Darwinism*. Amersham, Buckingham: Avebury, 1981. Print.

Brown Douglas. *Thomas Hardy*. London: Longmans, 1961. Print.

Buell, Lawrence. *The Future of Environmental Ecocriticism: Environmental Crisis and Literary Imagination*. USA: Blackwell Publishing, 2005. Print.

Bullen J.B. *The Expressive Eye: Fiction and Perception in the Work of Thomas Hardy*. Oxford: Clarendon Press, 1986. Print.

Burton, Richard. *Masters of the English Novel: A Study of Principles and Personalities*. Egypt: Library of Alexandria, 1909. Print.

Capra Fritjof. *The Web of Life*. London: Flamingo, 1997. Print.

Cecil, Lord David, *Hardy the Novelist.* Indianapolis: Bobb Merrill Company, 1946. Print.

Cheryll Glottfelty and Harold Fromm (eds.) *The Ecocriticism Reader: Landmarks in Literary Ecology.* Georgia: The University of Georgia Press, 1996.

Dave, Jagdish Chandra. *The Human Predicament in Hardy's Novels.* UK: Palgrave Macmillan, 1985. Print.

Dorothy Van Ghent, *The English Novel: Form and function.* New York: Harper and Row,2003. Print.

Draper, Ronald P. Thomas Hardy: The Tragic Novels. London: Palgrave Macmillan Ltd., 1991. Print.

Duffin, Henry Charles . *Thomas Hardy,* New Delhi: Anmol Publications 2000. Print.

Enstice, Andrew. *Thomas Hardy: Landscapes of the Mind.* London: Macmillan, 1979. Print.

Fanon Franz. *The Wretched of the Earth.* Trans. Richard Philcox. New York: Grove Press, 2004.

Frederick L.Gwynn and Joseph L.Blotner eds. *Faulkner in the University.* Virginia: University Press of Virginia, 1995. Print.

Garrard, Greg. *Ecocriticism.* New York: Routledge Taylor & Francis Group, 2012. Print.

Gittings Robert. *Young Thomas Hardy.* London: Penguin Books Limited, 1987. Print.

Grimsditch, Herbert B. *Character and Environment in the novels of Thomas Hardy.*New York: Haskell House, 1966. Print.

Guerard, Albert J. *Thomas Hardy: The Novels and Stories.* Cambridge: Harvard University Press, 1949.

Hardy, Florence Emily. *The Early Life of Thomas Hardy 1840 – 1891.* New York: Cambridge University Press, 2011.

Harvey, Geoffrey. *The Complete Critical Guide to Thomas Hardy.* New York: Routledge, 2003. Print.

Howe, Irving. *Thomas Hardy.* London: Palgrave Macmillan, 1985. Print.

John Holloway. *The Victorian Sage.* London. Macmillan & Co. Ltd. 1953. Print.

Johnson, Lionel. The Art of Thomas Hardy. London: John Lane The Bodley Head Ltd., 1923. Print.

Kramer, Dale, ed. *The Cambridge Companion to Thomas Hardy.* Cambridge: Cambridge University Press, 1999. Print.

Lawrence, D. H. *Phoenix: The Posthumous Papers of D. H. Lawrence*.New York: The Viking Press, 1936. Print.

Lawrence, D.H. *Study of Thomas Hardy and Other Essays*. London: Grafton Books, 1986. Print.

Love, A. Glenn. Practical Ecocriticism: Literature, Biology and the Environment. Charlottesville and London: University of Virginia Press, 2003. Print.

Manavalan. *Ayvu Sikalhalum Theervuhalum*. Chennai: International Institute of Tamil Studies, 1995. Print.

Mangaiyarkarasai S. *Ki.Ra.vin Sirugathai Padaipalumai*. Chennai: Kavya, 2003. Print.

Meera, ed. *Rajanarayaneeyam*. Sivagangai: Annam Publications Pvt. Ltd., 1985. Print.

Meera, comp. *Ki. Ra. Kadithangal*. Sivagangai: Annam Publications Pvt. Ltd., 1989. Print.

Merchant, Carolyn. *Earthcare: Women and the Environment* . London: Routhledge, Inc, 1996. Print.

---. *The Death of Nature: Women, Ecology, and the Scientific Revolution*. New York: Harper Collins, 1980. Print.

Merryn, Williams. *Thomas Hardy and Rural England*.London: Macmillan, 1974. Print.

Mill, John Stuart. *Three Essays on Religion*. New York: Cosmo Classics, 2008. Print.

Millgate, Michael and Purdy R.L. Ed. *The Collected Letters of Thomas Hardy*. Four Volumes. Oxford: The Clarendon Press, 1978 – 84. Print.

Millgate, Michael, Ed. *The Life and Work of Thomas Hardy by Thomas Hardy*. London: Macmillan, 1984. Print.

Millgate, Michael. *Thomas Hardy: A Biography Revisited*. Oxford: Oxford University Press, 2004. Print.

Mohit K. Ray. *Studies in Literary Criticism*. New Delhi: Atlantic Publishers and Distributors, 2002. Print.

Morgan, Rosemarie. *Women and Sexuality in the Novels of Thomas Hardy*. New York: Routledge, 1988. Print.

Murphy D. Patrick. *Literature, Nature and Other: Ecofeminist Critiques*. New York: State University of New York Press. 1995. Print.

Murugaiyyan Aranaga M., Murugan R. and P. Saravanankumar, eds. *Ki. Ra-vin Padaipugal:Aaivu Katturaigal*. Puducherry: Ilakkiya Pathipagam, 2002. Print.

Naess, Arne. *Ecology, Community and Lifestyle*. Trans. David Rothenberg. Cambridge: Cambridge University Press, 1989. Print.

Neill, S. Diana. *A Short History of the English Novel*. London: Collier Books, 1964. Print.

Noorul Hasan. *Thomas Hardy: The Sociological Imagination*. The Macmillan Press Ltd. London: 1982. Print.

Page, Norman, ed. *Oxford Reader's Companion to Hardy*. Oxford: Oxford University Press, 2000. Print.

Page, Norman. *Thomas Hardy: The Novels*. New York: Palgrave Macmillan, 2001. Print.

Panchangam K. *Maruvasippil Ki. Rajanarayanan*. Sivakangai. Annam Pvt. Ltd., 1996. Print.

Panchangam K. *Ki.Rajanarayananin Punaikathaigalum Iyarkkai Ezhuthuthalum*: Thanjavur: Annam, 2012. Print.

Pinion. F.B. *A Hardy Companion: A Guide to the Works of Thomas Hardy and their Background*. New York: Palgrave Macmillan, 1968. Print.

Plietzsch, Birgit. *The Novels of Thomas Hardy as a product of Nineteenth Century, Social, Economic, and Cultural Change*.Berlin: Tenea, 2004. Print.

Rabbets John. *From Hardy to Faulkner Wessex to Yokhnapatawpha*. New York: Palgrave Macmillan, 1989. Print.

Rajanarayanan, Ki. *Karisal Kaattu Kaduthasi*. Sivagangai: Annam Publications Pvt. Ltd. 1988. Print.

Rajanarayanan, Ki. *Ki. Rajanarayanan Kathaigal*, Thanjavur: Agaram, 2012. Print.

Rajanarayanan, Ki. *Ki.Rajanarayanan Katturaigal* (Ki. Rajanarayanan's Essays). Thanjavur:Agaram, 2011. Print.

Rajanarayanan, Ki. comp. *Karisal Kathaigal*.Thanjavur: Annam Pvt. Ltd., 2012. Print.

Rajanaryananan, Ki. *Ki.Ra. vin Pathilgal*: Thanjavur: Annam Pvt. Ltd., 2012. Print.

Rama Kundu ed. *Thomas Hardy: A Critical Spectrum*. New Delhi: Atlantic Publishers and Distributors, 2002. Print.

Ruth Firor. *Folkways in Thomas Hardy*. New York: A.S.Barnes and Company Inc., 1962. Print.

Selvamony Nirmal, Nirmaldasan and Rayson K. Alex, eds. *Essays in Ecocriticism*. OSLE India Chennai & Sarup & Sons, New Delhi: 2007. Print.

Sivaramakrishnan Muralai and Ujjwal Jana. Ecological *Criticism for Our Times: Literature, Nature and Critical Inquiry*. New Delhi: Authorspress, 2011. Print.

Shanmugasundaram K. and K. Panchangam. *Ki. Ra. 80: An Anthology of Essays on Ki. Ra*. Chennai: Kavya Publishers, 2002. Print.

Southerington, F.R. *Hardy's Vision of Man*. London. Chatto and Windus, 1971. Print.

Sturgeon, Noel. *Ecofeminist Natures: Race, Gender, Feminist Theory, and Political Action*. New York: Routhledge, 1997. Print.

Varadharajan M. *The Treatment of Nature in Sangam Literature*. Tirunelveli: The South India Saiva Siddhanta Works Publishing Society Ltd. 1969. Print.

Vijayalatchumi Rajaram. *Vattara Ilakkiyamum Ki.Rajanarayananum*. Sivakangai: Agaram Publications, 1995. Print.

Warren, Karen C. *Ecofeminism: Women, Culture, Nature.* Indiana: Indiana University Press, 1997. Print.

Weber, Carl J. *Hardy of Wessex.* New York: Columbia University Press, 1940. Print.

Webster, Harvey Curtis. *On a Darkling Plain*. Chicago: The University of Chicago Press, 1947. Print.

Wellek, Rene and Austin Warren. *Theory of Literature*. New York: Penguin, 1949. Print.

Wilkinson Sherren. *The Wessex of Romance*. London: Francis Griffiths, 1908.Print.

Williams, Raymond. *The English Novel from Dickens to Lawrence.* Oxford: Oxford University Press, 1970. Print.

Articles

Alex, K.Rayson. "A Survey of the Phases of Indian Ecocriticism." *CLC Web: Comparative Literature and Culture.* Vol.16, No.4. Article 9. Print.

Bates, Ernest Sutherland. "*The Optimism of Thomas Hardy.*" *International Journal of Ethics,* Vol. 15, No. 4 (Jul., 1905), pp. 469-485. Print.

Bate, Jonathan. "*Culture and Environment: From Austen to Hardy.*" *New Literary History,* Vol. 30, No. 3, Ecocriticism (Summer, 1999), pp. 541-560. Print.

Bennett, Barbara. "*Through Ecofeminist Eyes: Le Guin's "The Ones Who Walk Away from Omelas".*" *The English Journal.*July 2005. 63-68. Print.

Birch, B.P. "*Wessex, Hardy and the Nature Novelists.*" *Transactions of the Institute of British Geographers,* New Series, Vol. 6, No. 3 (1981), pp. 348-358.

Cornwell Margery and Robinson. "*OF COWS AND CATFISH: The Reading of Nature byThomas Hardy and Loren Eiseley.*" *Soundings: An Interdisciplinary Journal,* Vol. 68, No. 1 (Spring 1985), pp. 52-61. Print.

Cuthberton, Guy. "*Thomas Hardy's Vision of Wessex by Simon Gatrell.*" *The Review of English Studies,* New Series, Vol. 56, No. 223 (Feb., 2005), pp. 158-159. Print.

Darby, H.C. "*The Regional Geography of Thomas Hardy's Wessex.*" *Geographical Review,* Vol. 38, No. 3 (Jul., 1948), pp. 426-443. Print.

Gilbert, Neiman. "*Was Hardy Anthropomorphic?.*" *Twentieth Century Literature,* Vol. 2, No. 2 (Jul., 1956), pp. 86-91. Print.

Gregor, Ian. "Hardy's World." *ELH,* Vol. 38, No. 2 (Jun., 1971), pp. 274-293. Print.

Hyde, William J. "*Hardy's View of Realism: A Key to the Rustic Characters.*" *Victorian Studies,* Vol. 2, No. 1 (Sep., 1958), pp. 45-59. Print.

Jann, Rosemary. "*Hardy's Rustics and the Construction of Class.*" *Victorian Literature and Culture,* Vol. 28, No. 2 (2000), pp. 411-425. Print.

Jarret, David. "*Eustacia Vye and Eula Varner, Olympians: The Worlds of Thomas Hardy and William Faulkner.*" *NOVEL: A Forum on Fiction*, Vol. 6, No. 2 (Winter, 1973), pp. 163-174. Print.

Knickerbocker Frances Wentworth. "The Victorianness of Thomas Hardy." *The Sewanee Review*, Vol. 36, No. 3 (Jul., 1928), pp. 310-325. Print.

Naess, Arne. 1973. "The Shallow and the Deep, Long-Range Ecology Movement: A Summary." Inquiry: An Interdisciplinary Journal of Philosophy and the Social Sciences 16: 95–100.

Naess, Arne. 1986. "The Deep Ecology Movement: Some Philosophical Aspects." Philosophical Inquiry 8: 10–31.

Neiman, Gilbert. "*Thomas Hardy, Existentialist.*" *Twentieth Century Literature*, Vol. 1, No. 4 (Jan., 1956), pp. 207-214. Print.

Phelps, William Lyon. "*The Novels of Thomas Hardy.*" *The North American Review*, Vol. 190, No. 647 (Oct., 1909), pp. 502-514. Print.

Richards, Caroline Mary. "Thomas Hardy's Ironic Vision. Part Two." "*Nineteenth-Century Fiction*," Vol. 4, No. 1 (Jun., 1949), pp. 21-35. Print.

Smart, Alastair. "*Pictorial Imagery in the Novels of Thomas Hardy.*" *The Review of English Studies*, New Series, Vol. 12, No. 47 (Aug., 1961), pp. 262-280. Print.

William Newton, A. Oklahoma and M. College. "*Hardy and the Naturalists: Their Use of Physiology.*" *Modern Philology*, Vol. 49, No. 1 (Aug., 1951), pp. 28-41. Print.

Printed by Libri Plureos GmbH in Hamburg,
Germany